From S
to
Stratford

by

William Peter Robinson

Further copies of this book may be obtained from:
W. P. Robinson, Bakery House, The Green, Chartham, Canterbury, Kent CT4 7JW.

ISBN-10: 0-9551294-0-0
ISBN-13: 978-0-9551294-0-7

Published, typeset, printed and bound by
Cupit Print, The Ropewalk, 23 Louth Road, Horncastle, Lincs., LN9 5ED.
Telephone: 01507 522339, Fax: 01507 525438, www.cupits.com

Cover picture shows Carnforth Steam Depot with an insert of The Cockney Sparrow which was Stratford Diesel Depot's logo.

Preface

This book relates to the working practices and conditions in the maintenance of locos, both steam and diesel, on the railway. The author began work as an apprentice fitter at Carnforth Motive Power Depot in the early nineteen sixties. Over the course of several years he worked at Carlisle and Crewe and later moved South and worked at Marylebone, Camden, Willesden and Cricklewood. After many years working as a fitter in the sheds he fulfilled his ambition and became the youngest full-time breakdown foreman on the railway at Stratford. During this time he attended over three thousand, seven hundred derailments in the South East.

Acknowledgements

Thanks must go to my family who accepted my sudden and sometimes very prolonged periods of absence with, usually, good nature (especially on pay day). Also the hard working gang who gave me unfailing loyalty and support and endured the most arduous conditions with good nature. Thank you to Nobby Richardson from the Cricklewood and Old Oak Common gang who, latterly, spent many hours assisting me when my memory loss took over. I also wish to mention my appreciation of York Railway Museum for their help in finding the track plans and cover photograph, The Science Museum in West London and Stratford Library, Steve Newton of Cupit Print for his help and advice. And lastly, special thanks must go to Barry Herbert, retired publisher, whose enthusiasm and encouragement has helped bring the book to fruition.

Introduction

My career of forty two years, working initially for British Rail and then English Welsh and Scottish railway, has taken me from Carnforth, as an apprentice fitter, to Carlisle, Marylebone, Crewe, Cricklewood and Stratford and a few more places besides. Initially I never dreamed I would end up in charge of one of the busiest and most respected breakdown gangs in the country. The railway has undergone many changes during this time and this is an account of some of my experiences, an insight into the working practices of years ago and some of the working conditions which are so different to those nowadays.

I should have been a farmer but my Father wanted me to get myself a trade before going on the land. As you will see, I never did go back to farming. Although the work on the railway was dirty, hard and heavy, it was much easier than hill farming and, as I was used to working long hours during the lambing season or hay time, the long hours on the railway didn't bother me.

William Peter Robinson

CHAPTER 1
CARNFORTH

I started on the railway in the early '60s at Carnforth Motive Power Depot as an apprentice diesel fitter, one of the first in the days of steam. I had never intended to work on the railway as I had no interest in it. I didn't even collect loco numbers. I was going to be a farmer but my father wanted me to get a trade first before going on the land. I had written off to heavy engineering companies looking for employment as a fitter or turner apprentice and was waiting for a reply. My older sister, who had been recently married, visited us with her husband and his father. During the afternoon Mr. Burgess, my sister's father-in-law, asked me what I was going to do and when I told him that I was looking for an apprenticeship in engineering he told me to go to Carnforth and see Harry Bolton in the railway shed. He was the foreman there. As I had nothing to do the next day, I took a train from Lancaster Castle station to Carnforth. I was told how to get to the shed from the station by platform staff and eventually found myself outside the doors to No. 1 road. I looked into the shed and was amazed at the size of the engines and how dark and dirty everything looked. I walked inside trying not to touch anything and was eventually asked what I wanted. My reply was that I would like to see Harry Bolton. I was taken into the workshop and introduced to him. He was very busy and, when I asked if there were any vacancies for apprentices, he told me there were not. Then he said that he knew all the lads who lived at Carnforth and didn't recognise me. I told him I was from Lancaster. He wanted to know who told me to try Carnforth for a job. I told him it was Mr. Burgess. He asked if it was Colonel Burgess who worked on the railway and I said that it was. I was taken to an office and sat down. Harry took my school report away with him and someone brought me a cup of coffee and a chocolate biscuit. After a while Harry came back and said that an apprentice had just blinded himself, so there was a vacancy and when could I start.

Carnforth

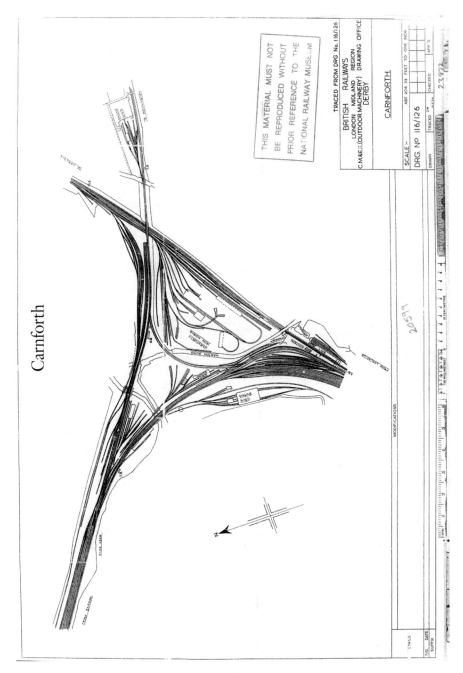

TRACED FROM DRG No 116/126

BRITISH RAILWAYS
LONDON MIDLAND REGION
C.M.&E.E (OUTDOOR MACHINERY) DRAWING OFFICE
DERBY

CARNFORTH

SCALE :- ABT 208 33 FEET TO ONE INCH

DRG. No 116/126

I told him next Monday, and he said that I would have to have a medical within a few weeks but to turn up at 0800 next Monday. I was to be a railway man. It wasn't what you knew but who you knew, Colonel Burgess was the Superintendent of the North West area of the railway. Initially, I worked mostly in the Carnforth shed. I had to attend night school at Lancaster and Morecambe College of Further Education for one night a week.

Access to the shed was via a long foot bridge that spanned the ten or twelve roads between the station and the shed. I only saw the bridge used by visitors or ambulance men as all the fitting and footplate staff would walk over the tracks. Carnforth was a through shed, six roads wide with deep pits. The walls, roof and pillars were caked in soot about an inch thick.

The shed was in operation twenty four hours a day, seven days a week, with about twenty fitters on the day shift along with one electrician, a blacksmith, a white metaller and a brick arch man. The boiler smiths would keep themselves to themselves. I think there were about half a dozen on each shift with their mates. On the back shift and night shift there were fewer staff but all sorts of repairs and exams were carried out. I was the newest of five apprentices, the oldest was actually working as a fitter with his own tools.

In the summer, when the sun was shining through small holes in the roof, fingers of bright sunlight would pierce the gloom and, if the asbestos lagging round a boiler was disturbed or being renewed, tiny iridescent blue particles would be seen swirling about in the air (very dangerous, as we now know.)

The workshop was alongside the middle of No.1 road, by the drop pit. The walls and floors of the pits were brick built with the rails running along the top and the depth of the pits was about four feet.

In the workshop, all the machines were belt driven. A long spindle, to which the machines were attached, ran the length of the shop and the belts would flap about. If one came off its wheel, and that happened often, it would get caught in another and pull that one off and so on. We had to be quick to shut off the spindle or knock our machine out of gear.

On my second day at Carnforth, an incident took place that would steer my railway career towards breakdown work, re-railing and rescue.

A ten ton loaded coal wagon was being lifted up to the top of the coal bunker to be tipped at the top. The rails went up with the wagon as if on a massive fork lift and this left a large hole which the next wagon rolled into, jamming the machinery which was lifting the wagon. The shunter had not secured the wagon's hand brake.

As the elevated wagon was not high enough to get the jib of the breakdown crane underneath, and central to lift the offending wagon out of the hole, it had to be jacked out and all available staff worked on this.

The hand jacks were old water type jacks which leaked at every stroke and had to be topped up regularly with a watering can. The packing which went under the wagon to hold it up was new sleepers and we used a wagon load of them. Because we worked under the coal bunker, the coal dust was thick and got everywhere. Everyone had black faces and the whites of their eyes and teeth shone in contrast.

I was quite strong and fit, so I was lifting the jacks and sleepers along with the grown ups and good banter was being hurled about, and I seemed to fit in with the gang so easily. I went home very tired and black as coal. Fortunately, we were supplied with three pairs of overalls, one in the wash, one to work in, and the cleanest to wear to travel to and from work.

At Carnforth there was only one cold water tap for washing and that was outside. Everyone would get a handful of sand and a handful of oil and we would use the mixture to clean our hands then wipe them with a rag, an ideal way to end up with dermatitis, which I did.

With so much Welsh steam coal about, it was easy to find fossilised leaves and ferns in the large cobs of coal. Some of the lumps of coal in the tenders were far too big to go in the fire box and the fireman had to break them up into manageable lumps. Sometimes I would gently break up a large piece across the grain and there would be the shape of a fern as delicate as it was on the day it had been growing millions of years ago.

That first week I saw my first fatality. It was lunchtime and some of us were sitting on a bench at the south end of the shed eating sandwiches in the sun. Because of the lack of washing facilities, we would take a piece of paper big enough to go round our sandwich and eat it without touching the bread with our dirty hands. Mother's Pride sliced loaf wrapper was the most used.

A steam raiser, who was responsible for lighting the fires in the locos that were due to depart the shed and make sure that there was enough steam pressure, was coming over to us, jumping over the pits and a loco was clanking towards us. The driver was looking out of the left side and cheeking us. He didn't see the chap on the right. The steam raiser jumped and slipped in front of the loco which went over him, the wheels cutting him in two. There was very little blood as the weight of the loco had almost sealed the two halves. One of the old fitters, Gary, said, "He was a good bloke, he was", and bit into his sandwich. I threw up and began to wonder what sort of job I was getting into.

My wages for 48 hours, 6 days a week, were 26 shillings or £1.30p a week, with 6 old pence in tax. The hours were reduced to 44 a week whilst I was there. The obvious thing would be to work just a four hour shift on the Saturday but the railway decided we would work a full shift every second Saturday. So we worked 40 hours the first week and 48 the second. This was for only a short period because the weekly hours came down again to 42 and then 40 at which it stayed for many years.

The day came when I was to have my medical. The eyesight test was a bit worrying and it was decided I would need spectacles but, when it came to the colour blind test, I almost made a mess of it.

I was given a book with loads of dots on each page, I had never seen this test before and when the doctor asked me what number I could see, I answered three, the number at the bottom of the page. After he explained that there was a number hidden in the dots, I was fine.

Everyone was supplied with clogs, I was told that they were made by prisoners so the railway got them cheap. For a shilling, one of the fitters' mates would remove the corkers from the bottom (they were like horse shoes) and fit a shaped piece of rubber car tyre in their place. It made everyone two inches taller and safer when working round the framing of the steam locos. Before I had my clogs refurbished with the tyres, I was working on a steam valve on the side of a loco boiler and a boiler smith was gas welding below me. As I came to turn round, I found my clogs had been welded to the framing of the loco. I had to take my feet out of the clogs and go and find a hammer and chisel to remove the clogs from the framing. Because of all the water lying about the floor, I went home with wet socks that day.

As the youngest apprentice, I was the butt of many jokes and much ribbing. One of the silly things I was sent to the stores for was a 'long stand'. The store man told me to wait then disappeared. After a half hour wait I was becoming more and more worried, then he returned and told me I had had my long stand and should get back to my fitter. I was annoyed with myself for falling for that one, but I still ended up going back to the stores for 'buckets of steam' and 'sky hooks' but it was a happy shed to work in.

When removing a set of wheels from a steam loco, and it was usually the driving wheels, all the connecting rods and brake rigging were uncoupled first, then the horn stays. The horn stays were fastened to the bottom of the horns which were perpendicular and the axle boxes on the wheel sets could slide up and down them. Once everything was removed, the loco was shunted on to the drop pit which was about twelve feet long and made of steel. The wheels which were to be removed were positioned in the middle of the drop pit and securely scotched because all the brake rigging had been removed and, therefore, there were no brakes on the loco.

The drop pit would be gently lowered, the complete section of steel pit and rails would be dropped down about ten feet, taking the wheel set with it. Two rails were slid into position, one on either side, and locked into position. The loco could then be shunted out of the way and the rails which had bridged the gap would be unlocked and slid to one side clearing the gap. The drop pit could then be lifted up with the wheels free to be removed for turning or re-profiling. The only problem with the old hydraulic drop pit at Carnforth was that it would stop two inches from the top and had to be manually pumped up the remaining distance before it could be locked into position.

I listened to the breakdown gang discussing derailments which they had been on and found it interesting and I would join in the conversation, asking questions and showing interest. Because of my strength and cheek, the gang would encourage me to try and get permission to go out with them. However, as an apprentice, I was not allowed to work overtime. Harry Bolton, the foreman, eventually gave in and let me go out with the gang but I had to be back at Carnforth to clock off at the right time. The arrangement didn't last for long because it was a nuisance getting me back every time. A compromise was struck. I was allowed to clock off by 'phone, usually at Lancaster Castle Station, my home station. Soon after this I was allowed another concession. I was allowed to clock on by 'phone from Lancaster and be told where they were working and go and meet them on site. It was not long before I was getting a list of purchases to make to take to the gang, Woodbines and Weights cigarettes, Golden Virginia and Old Holborn tobacco and papers and newspapers. Because I was so poorly paid, the foreman, usually Harry Bolton, would tell me not to give any change as they all worked very long hours and were on good money. No one minded and I profited by it.

One of the first jobs I was allowed on was a Midland tanky engine that had derailed and rolled down a bank. This was on a high bank that went round the Giant Axe playing field by Lancaster Castle station. It was a single line and had a very tight curve with a six inch cant. It ran to Glasson Dock. When we arrived, the loco was half way down the bank with its wheels in the air and resting on a telegraph pole. We didn't know if the pole was holding it or not, so everybody had to stay above it. The only way to make it safe was to lasso the telegraph pole and, with a long rope, pull it away from the loco. As it moved, so did the loco and completed its roll to the bottom. From the top to the bottom of the bank it had done a complete turn and landed on its wheels. This was now safe for us to work on, but the bodies of the driver and fireman had to be taken away first. The coal had spilled out of the tender and trapped them against the front of the boiler and firebox door.

As the crane was standing on a six inch cant and lifting on the low side, the outriggers had to be set with great care and I learnt how to make a crane safe in what could be dangerous conditions. The strange thing is, I have picked up quite a few cranes that have gone over and most of them were on jobs that were safe, but the crane was not set up correctly or the foreman had not looked at the ground he was packing on. If a crane is set up well and bedded down with the packing under the outriggers then liberties can be taken with it, but only small ones.

It was about this time a new innovation for the track was being tried out, just south of Lancaster; welded rail. Instead of the clickity clack of the wheels passing over the joints every sixty feet there was no noise at all. To avoid the rails buckling in the heat of summer, every quarter of a mile was an expansion joint or breather. Instead of the rail butting up to the next one, the ends of the rails were tapered. This enabled the rails to slide against each other. Now all the main line is laid with welded rail.

All the breakdown gangs thought that they were the best and worked harder and quicker than the others and, in a pub, they may be. However, on site, skill and practice will soon show. The foreman, Harry Bolton, was a very careful breakdown man and taught me a great deal. Also, the crane drivers had years of experience and guarded their cranes jealously. Sometimes, on a job with lots of craning, one of the gang would look after the fire and water and keep the steam up. Travelling with the crane under its own power or raising and lowering the jib would use up steam pressure rapidly and the amount of water injected into the boiler had to be gauged just right or steam pressure would be lost very quickly. If too much cold water was put in the boiler at one time, the steam pressure would drop and the job would stop and everyone would be waiting for the water to heat up and make steam. On a tandem lift, if one of the crane drivers said he was building up steam and was not ready when asked, he would incur the wrath of the foreman and mickey-taking from the lads on the floor and, much worse, from the other gang.

I was often asked to help the crane driver and learnt the tricks of crane driving. Also, I learned how to keep the ash pan clean to give a good draught into the fire box but it could only be cleaned out when we were slewed round so that the ash would go on to the track and not the relieving bogie.

The fitters received six old pence a day which was known as 'hot and cold' money. This was for working on locos that were in steam where everything was very hot or very cold and wet. The fitters also received an extra six old pence a day examining money. This enabled the railway to hold something over anyone who missed seeing something wrong. A fitter could find a dozen things wrong but if he missed one thing, even a minor fault, he would end up with a 'please explain' letter and that would go on his record.

When a fitter was examining a loco, the only aids he had were either a 'Smokey Joe' or a carbide lamp. The Smokey Joe was a basic Aladdin's lamp with a spout. It was filled with signal oil, a rough paraffin, with an asbestos wick down the spout which was then lit. There was more smoke than light. Some of the fitters would make their own version of this out of tin plate. One old fitter had a small teapot. The carbide lamp had two portions, the bottom half held carbide rocks and small chippings and on the top there was a small water tank with a drip tap into the bottom. When the water dripped on to the rocks of carbide, a gas was given off which was flammable. A small stem came out from the bottom chamber, up the side to the top of the water tank with a valve to regulate the gas flow. It all stood about eight inches high with a handle off set at the top so as not to burn the user's hand. The water was allowed to drip for a few minutes then the valve was opened and the gas lit. Some of these lamps would have a small circular mirror behind the flame to increase the light. If the water was set dripping and the valve was not open, the lamp would explode quite violently and blow the top and bottom apart. The only person to have a battery operated torch was the electrician. He had to look after the A.W.S. batteries and a naked flame was too dangerous to use near them.

The workshop I mentioned earlier was approached through big double doors from the drop pit and the first thing to see was the wheel lathe. This could take a ten foot high pair of driving wheels for re-profiling the tyres. A gantry ran from the drop pit to the wheel lathe and a pulley block system was used to lift the wheel set from the drop pit and position it in the centres of the wheel lathe. It was about fifty feet from the double doors to the back wall which had high windows which were impossible to see through because of the thick layer of soot which covered them. All along the back walls were the belt driven lathes, drilling machines, shaping machines and borers. On the left hand side, backing on to the side wall, was the white metaller's hearth. This was gas fired and always warm in the winter. Immediately opposite, eighty feet away on the other side wall, was the blacksmith's forge. This was where I learnt to use big hammers weighing fourteen and twenty eight pounds. If the blacksmith's striker was off or helping someone else, I would strike for him. I soon managed to get the swing right and the secret was not to take my eyes off the place meant to be struck. The smith always would say, "I nod my head and you hit it". Luckily, I knew what he meant.

I would often stand by the white metal hearth watching the ingots of white metal de-form into a mercury-like pool.

The hearth had two big cast iron pots set in flush and each one would take four or five ingots to fill it. As they melted, a multi-coloured skin would form over the top, much brighter than petrol on water.

Every morning the fitting staff would congregate round the warm hearth and the leading hand would bring the work sheets and repair cards out and distribute them to the assembled staff and inform the apprentices who they were to work with or which other jobs they would be trusted with to work alone.

One day, and luckily it was in the middle of the afternoon, a water tank situated in the roof above the white metal hearth sprung a leak and water poured on to the hearth and into the molten white metal. The result was a massive explosion throwing molten metal everywhere and a thick steam making it impossible to see. I was in the shed when this happened, as were most of the staff. We all ran into the workshop and found the white metaller very badly burned and a young fitter who had been drilling on the large column drill also badly burned. They were both rushed to hospital. I saw the fitter again but the white metaller did not return to work before I left to go to work in Carlisle some time later.

On a big exam, the pistons, valves, side rods and cross heads all had to be removed. The pistons and valves were fitted with new rings. The side rods and driving rods had their brass bearings pressed out and re-metalled, then machined to size. The bearings were all skimmed to almost fit the journals then finished off with a scraper. Each bearing had to be correct and offered up to the journal before being pressed into the driving and side rods. The journals stuck out of the wheels about half way down the spokes and took all the force from the pistons, turning linear motion to circular motion. The valves looked like a set of weights which a weight lifter would use. The centre spindle was about four feet long with the actual valves close to the ends. These were wide enough to take four or five rings. The rings were steel and had to be fitted to the valve. In each ring groove was a small spigot. One end of the ring would be butted up to this and any overhang or surplus would be marked off, then the ring would be removed and the surplus would be cut off and a groove filed in the end to fit the spigot. When all the rings were the correct length and before the valve was replaced into the steam chest, the rings were fitted and, as they would spring open slightly, it was difficult to position the valves in place without breaking a ring on the inside ports. A repair card would be placed under the two ends of the ring and tapped gently down into place. This would hold the ring tight in the groove and would be easier to fit into the steam chest. One day, I was doing this prior to fitting the valves when the shed master came up behind me wanting to know what I was doing. I told him and received a great amount of verbal abuse as this was a practice that was frowned upon because the card under intense heat turned into carbon. None of the fitters had told me this so I had to stand there and take it. I was still a bit green then.

The valves would be about ten inches across. The pistons would be anything up to twenty four inches across but with only the one lump to fit the rings to and only two rings. They were awkward to fit. The rings could be pushed down with the finger tips as the piston was slid into place, getting one's finger ends out of the way before losing a nail was an art form.

On a loco that had inside motion it would be almost impossible to see if the bearings were over heating, so a garlic bomb was fitted close to the bearings. It was a cylinder about three inches long and an inch across, which fitted into a recess and was secured. Inside the tube was a garlic smelling substance and that was sealed in with a sort of pitch that would only melt at very high temperatures. If a bearing started to run hot, the seal on the tube would melt and the strong smell would escape. It was such a strong vile smell that the footplate staff could easily smell it, even going at full speed. Occasionally these garlic bombs had to be changed and now and again one would be left on the back of the white metaller's hearth, and the smell would clear the workshop of staff and the stink would linger for days.

Another safety feature was the fusible plug. On the inside of the fire box the plugs would be fitted. The middle of the plug was filled with lead, and if the water in the boiler dropped to a dangerous level the lead would melt and the water from the boiler would flow into the fire box. It wouldn't put out the fire, but would indicate to the footplate staff that they had a problem and the fire could be put out or dropped.

Another thing, on the big exams we had to clean the sieves in the tender by the injectors. They were about twelve inches by nine inches and filtered the water from the tender to the boiler. To get to them we had to enter the tender at the back. On the top was a kind of manhole and we would make our way through the baffles to the front. Although the tender had been drained it was always wet with two inches of water on the bottom and sometimes fish would be flapping about and hundreds of silver fish were in there. With only a smoky lamp with a very dim yellow light we invariably put our hands on to something slimy. This was always the apprentices' job and any other apprentice who knew someone was in there would bang on the side with a big hammer which made such a din. It was like being inside a bell. Also they would throw smouldering rags in through the manhole to make it even more uncomfortable. It was bad enough with a smoky lamp.

Once we had disconnected the sieves, they would be put on a fire, then scrubbed with a wire brush and the whole thing had to be gone through again to replace them. The fish in the tender got there by being scooped up out of the water troughs which were situated between the rails. As the train sped along the track, the fireman had to wind a handle which was connected to the scoop situated under the tender. The scoop had to be dropped at just the right moment, otherwise ballast and bits of wooden sleeper would be scooped up and damage the scoop. The troughs were about fourteen inches wide, ten inches deep, and about half a mile long. If anyone was walking down the track by the side of one of these troughs they were liable to get drenched in water if a train went passed and dropped its scoop, but from a safe distance, it was an awesome sight to watch, seeing tons of water spraying out either side of the loco.

I soon learnt the card games played on the railway. Cribbage, and Three Card Brag and, if there was time, Solo. Solo whist and Crib were two games I had to learn very quickly. If I laid a wrong card I would receive a clip round the ear and verbal abuse. With Brag, I only lost money. Sometimes, to keep out of the sight of the foreman, we would play cards in a fire box using the brick arch as a table, but we had to be very dedicated as it was so uncomfortable and the cards very dirty and the light poor.

Above the fire box door at eye level were two gauge glasses that showed the water level in the boiler. They were protected by thick glass covers. The protection was not only to stop the footplate staff from breaking them but to protect the driver and fireman when they shattered, and that was often. One day in the shed one of the young fitters was on running repairs and was cleaning the covers. One of the gauge glasses exploded in his face and glass went into his eyes. An older fitter, Tom, had him lay down on a bench and produced a wickedly sharp knife which he used to scrape the glass from his eye balls. Once that was done, just to finish the job off, he licked both eyes with his tongue, and he made sure he couldn't feel any glass remaining. Surprisingly the young fitter had no after affects with his sight. Tom, who everyone thought had saved the young fitter's sight, suffered from boils on the back of his neck. One day he was in so much pain that one of the mates, Ben, would fix him. Tom was sat facing the back of a chair. Ben filled an empty milk bottle with steam from a degger pipe and put the top of the bottle over the boil. Then he put cold wet clothes over the bottle. This dropped the temperature in the bottle causing a vacuum. The idea was that the vacuum would draw the muck and puss out of the boil. It was a good idea but the boil wasn't ready to burst and one and a half inches of Toms neck was inside the neck of the bottle causing even more pain and the bottle had to be smashed to relieve the vacuum.

Ben, who had been unable to do an apprenticeship because of the First World War was a craftsman in his own right. He lived in the middle of Carnforth and had the attics of four shops that were in a square. In the attics he had built a model railway of about three inch gauge. He made the locos and rolling stock himself. The locos were steam powered, and sometimes he would bring into work a driving wheel he was working on after he had cast it and clean it up with a jeweller's tiny file during the lunch break.

One of the boiler smith's mates was called Bulldog. He was short and quite strong in the arm if not in the head. The young fitters would wind him up about his strength, and one day they bet him he couldn't lift his own body weight. He knew he could and thought he was to make some money. The fitters brought out a big bucket and told him to stand in it and lift himself up. He tried for a long time before he had to give up. And the next day he was going to try and do it with pulley blocks. One thing about Bulldog, he was always on the scrounge and if someone was rolling a cigarette, he would be there asking for one. It was the young fitters again who decided to try and change him. One of them had rolled horsehair, fibreglass and blue asbestos in a cigarette with just a bit of tobacco at the ends, and when Bulldog asked him for a roll-up he gave him the one that had been doctored. He was coughing and spluttering all afternoon but it didn't stop him from trying to smoke everybody else's cigarettes.

Some of the older fitters had been involved in the fighting in the war and were still affected by it. I was told to ask one of them if I could borrow his shoes. I declined this strange request but eventually, because the young fitters kept on at me, I did. I wasn't ready for his reaction. He flew into a rage and chased me round the shed brandishing a hammer, to everyone else's amusement.

I managed to stay out of his way for the rest of the day, and safe. The following day, all I received was a surly look from him. I found out later that he had been a prisoner of war and it had given him this kink about his shoes.

Another fitter had shell shock and loud bangs would set him off. Another apprentice banged on the side of a smoke box in which he was working. He jumped out, grabbed the apprentice and threw him in the smoke box, shutting the door. The loco was in steam and he opened the blast pipe. I think the apprentice had been put up to this because other fitters rushed to open the smoke box door and get him out before he died of asphyxia. Not everyone was mad but, as they said, "It did help" if you worked there.

The first winter was very cold and, as the shed ran north to south, the north wind would whistle through the shed straight from the Lake District. Frost fires would be lit by every loco being worked on and spanners and bars stood against the braziers to take the chill off the metal. A four foot bar would snap like a carrot if it was used to undo the cylinder cover nuts with a box spanner. In the depth of winter when it was at its coldest, number six road had fires lit in the pit along the full length and locos that had frozen up were placed along that road to thaw them out. It was a common sight to see steam blowing down on to the hand rail alongside the boiler, and instantly freezing, but it was wet steam.

One day the snow plough was called for. The plough was on sleepers at the end of one of the roads north of the shed. The buffers were removed from a loco and the loco driven up to the plough and bolted to the buffer beam. This was in a raging blizzard. No one ever thought to get the ploughs ready in good weather. Harry Bolton, the foreman, was standing watching the fitting of the plough which didn't go well because it had settled on the sleepers after it had been removed the year before and had to be lifted with bars and wedges to match the holes from plough to buffer beam. All Harry had on to combat the weather was his trilby hat and a blue smock. He was covered in snow. We were warm from physical work. Poor Harry came down with pneumonia and died soon afterwards, and a good foreman was lost to the railway because he wanted to see for himself that the plough was fitted properly.

I was usually working with a breakdown fitter on the large exams because when a breakdown call came, we would go over to the breakdown train and still leave fitting staff to carry on working on the exam. Often four or five fitters would be on the same exam which took days to complete. The breakdown train was like everything else on the shed, covered in oil and soot. The lighting was by paraffin oil lamps, tilly and floods and I learnt the art of tying and fitting mantels.

Because the capacity of the cranes was usually only forty to forty five tons, we would often assist other gangs with lifts. Even with the loco and tender split apart, the loco would be too heavy for only one crane to lift. We often would travel north into Carlisle's patch and they would come down to us, so I met them regularly on the bigger jobs and, when I moved up to Carlisle Upperby, I was accepted into their gang.

I had three accidents in the first year. I was struck on the head and laid out by a crosshead cotter. This was a piece of steel that fastened together the crosshead and the piston. It was about twelve inches long and shaped to fit the hole between crosshead and rod of the piston. It would be belted into position with big hammers and, when it had to be removed, it was always seized up and took a great deal of hammering and warming up with the cutting torch to remove it. Nothing was actually cut but the metal was warmed and expanded around the cotter pin to free it. The one that hit me was shot out from a loco on the road alongside the one I was working on and it caught me on the back of the head and knocked me out. We had no hard hats in those days. I came round, had a cup of tea and went back to work.

The second accident I had, again, involved splitting a piston rod from the crosshead. This time I was helping to knock out the crosshead cotter. I was with the fitter in the pit under the loco.

I was holding the dolly up between the wheels on to the bottom of the cotter pin and the fitter, Barry, was on the hammer, a long-shafted 14lb. He was a very large man and as strong as his size suggested and wielding a big hammer was no problem to him. As he struck the dolly it would jar in my hands and I started to aim the back of the dolly to the hammer. If I had kept my eyes shut I would have been safe but as it happened the hammer glanced off the dolly and struck my left wrist, smashing nine bones. I was off work for over three months. It was in the early summer and the weather, I remember, was good and putting up with a pot arm was no hardship.

The next accident I had could have been a lot worse but I was lucky. I was sitting on the top of the smoke box removing a damaged chimney. The loco was 43130. I had my back to the front of the loco with my legs splayed out around the smoke box. A loco was going off the shed from the road we were working on. It was four or five locos away and the driver was having trouble getting it to go forward. This often happened if the valves had stopped in the middle position. The steam would blow straight through, so the valves had to be reversed to get a slight bit of movement, then reversed again to go forward. The driver gave the loco too much steam in reverse and it shot into the one behind which hit the next one and so on, back to the one I was sitting on. 43130 was struck, not very hard but enough for me to go over backwards, striking my back on a buffer. Then I fell into the pit and, again, I was hospitalised. The X rays showed no broken bones but the muscles had been pushed out of place around my right shoulder blade. This took about six months of physiotherapy, three days a week in the afternoons at Lancaster Royal Infirmary. I was still working but not with the breakdown on these days.

One Saturday morning I had a near miss. A loco, Arethusa, was being prepared for a football special to take supporters from Morecambe to Blackpool for a cup game. Most of the staff were working on the loco. I was sitting on the floor with my legs over the rail between the wheels. I was rodding out the sand pipes. Sand would be blown by steam on to the rails under the wheels to give the loco better traction, and the sand pipes would often clog up with wet sand. I heard a loco buffering up to another and then another and, remembering the accident I had on 43130, I lifted my legs from between the wheels just as Arethusa was knocked back. The leg of my loose overalls was still over the rail and a wheel stopped on top of it. Fitters and cleaners were all jumping off the loco and shouting. The shed master heard the commotion and came out of his office. He saw what had happened and sacked the driver on the spot. One of the fitters moved the loco so that I could stand up with nothing more than a well creased leg on my overalls.

At Christmas all the fitters would have a collection for the apprentices as a Christmas box. All the money that had been collected over the weeks running up to Christmas Eve was put in a steel box about twelve inches square and welded shut, then all the apprentices, about five of us, would battle with the young fitters to get it off them. As the box was made of mild steel it was quite robust and stood up to much abuse. It was sometimes tossed into the forge or the bosh. The bosh was a big tank of water which the blacksmith used to cool down his hot metal. Most of the money was half crowns or florins. No one would put in a ten shilling or a pound note. It would take us most of the day before we eventually managed to get it, then with a hammer and chisel, it would be opened and the money shared out.

Because I attended night school and was quite good at technical drawing, I was asked to put some plans together for a car park at the north of the shed. This wasn't because the staff were obtaining cars, but the ambulance men were always complaining about going over the long footbridge. I thought I had done a good job with sleeper walls to hold back the ballast from the main line. But it meant that the main line to Barrow would have had to be slewed over about a foot.

This 45 ton steam crane (built in 1926 by Cowans Sheldon) is now on the North Yorkshire Moors' Railway and is typical of the breakdown crane used at Carnforth and Carlisle. *(Photograph courtesy of David Idle of North Yorkshire Moors' Railway).*

CHAPTER 2
CARLISLE

Because I was an apprentice diesel fitter and Carnforth had no allocation of diesels, only a shunting loco in the yard and the Metro Vics that would fail regularly in the station, I requested a transfer to Carlisle Upperby, which was granted almost immediately. The management must have been glad to see the back of me because I was a walking disaster and so accident prone. Funnily enough, I had no more accidents for a while but I did contract dermatitis soon after I arrived at Carlisle.

It had been arranged that I would travel to Carlisle on the Monday morning and report to the shed foreman on my arrival at Upperby. On arrival at Citadel station, Carlisle, I found Upperby was a good walk up London Road, so off I went and was surprised at the size of Carlisle as I had never been there before. I was told, "Turn right at the hill top, go passed the tannery and down the slope to the shed", and there it was, a great blue brick round house, with other sheds off it and alongside it.

I soon found the shed foreman and presented myself. He was very busy and told me to acquaint myself with Upperby and find somewhere cheap and cheerful to live. I found the cheap but not very cheerful. It was like a corrugated iron Nissen hut. No rooms but stalls with half doors in two rows facing each other down the length of the hut. The bed was three planks and these ran the full length of the wall through each stall. It cost nine pence a night. I stayed there the first night without even removing my shoes. When I left in the morning I took with me lots of livestock which took a while to lose. The second night, I slept in the cab of a Class 40. The foreman found out and made arrangements for me to stay in the railway hostel. This was really intended for double trip drivers and firemen only. Footplate crews would bring trains into Carlisle then stay the night or day and return to their home station and depot after having a rest. The hostel must have had

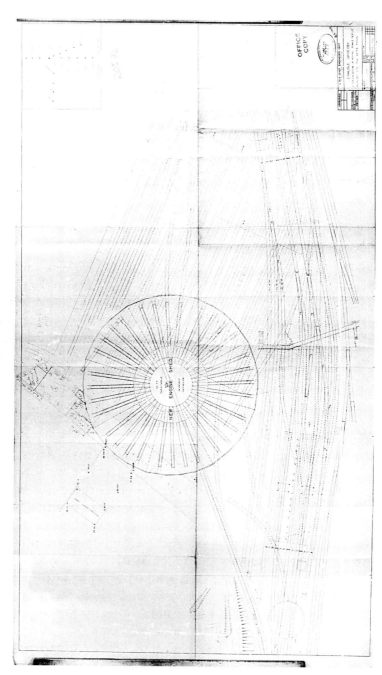

Carlisle

fifty or sixty bedrooms with a bed, stool, window and deep windowsill and a small cabinet with a Bible in the bottom. The windowsill made a good shelf. After my first night it felt like a palace. A handful of drivers were full time residents for different reasons. Some sad and some unlucky. Also there were road learners, usually in pairs, who came from other areas to learn the routes and railway around Carlisle. Sometimes as many as five or six pairs would be staying at one time and they stayed for about a month. If they found the state controlled beer to their liking they would take longer to learn the roads. The hostel was situated at the top of the slope to the right passed the tannery. In the summer the smell had to be experienced to be believed and everyone would rush passed holding their breath.

The messing and washing facilities at Upperby were brand-new and very good. A proper canteen with staff who would prepare hot food such as Cornish pasties, beans on toast, and toasted tea cakes, also bread pudding and sticky buns. The habit of cleaning most of the dirt off my hands with oil stayed with me and diesel oil was so effective at removing the dirt, followed by washing with green carbolic soap, similar to the kind my mother used to wash the floor. It was inevitable that I would suffer with dermatitis. That caused me to have another four weeks off work and I had been there barely a month.

I had a pal there, another apprentice from Carnforth, Mick. The two of us would be up, have our breakfast, and down to the shed. Every morning our first job was to carry out an A exam on the loco that would pull the 0800 depart from Carlisle to London, an English Electric Class 40. The A exam consisted of oil levels, brake block check, boiler run up and a good look round. The boiler was needed to heat the coaching stock as electric train heating was not built into the coaches. To fill the water tank to supply the boiler with water, a scoop had been fitted. It was hydraulic and would operate much more quickly than the steam locos winding down scoop. The fireman or driver's assistant, as they wanted to be called, would operate the lever for lowering the scoop at the same place on the track as they would have started to wind down the steam loco scoop and it would be down before reaching the troughs, hitting sleepers and ballast. This would smash the scoop and, on every exam, it would have to be changed. We kept our own supply and repaired any that could be repaired. It would take only minutes to change them over. The brake blocks had to be changed as and when required, not all twenty four at one time. The strange thing about the block behind the toilet pipe was that it never required changing. It seemed that all over the country everyone would blank off the air pipe to that individual cylinder with an old half penny to save themselves a dirty unpleasant job.

The food at the hostel was edible, just. There were kitchen staff on around the clock as footplate crews would be starting or finishing all through the day and night. On each shift there was a cook with an assistant, mostly old ladies. They did the best they could with the supplies they were given, I suppose, but the beef was always thin and fatty, the same as the soup and the breakfasts would today be called 'death by fat'.

There were never chips for dinner and Mick and me would complain to the cooks that we would like chips sometimes. We eventually wore them down and, one night as we went into the dining room, we were told by the cook that she would 'do some chips' for us. This was brilliant as it was only Mick and me who got them. All the drivers started to moan that we were getting preferential treatment but the ladies were hard as nails and soon quelled any uprising. We used this to our advantage. We told the cook on the morning shift that we had had chips made for us. The next day we, just Mick and I, had black pudding with the breakfast and, by playing one cook off the others, we started to eat very well. They would bring in titbits for us and stop off at the butcher on their way to work to try to better each other in their treatment of their young boys, with chips, black puddings, kidneys and fancy pastries. We enjoyed our food more and more. This would annoy the drivers but they would be at home the following day and we would be living there, as it seemed, for ever. It was all good hearted banter. A bit of cheek nearly always worked.

As all the drivers were top link men in their own depots, they were all getting on and most would rather drive a steam loco than a diesel. That was understandable as they knew every nut and bolt on a steam loco and how to get out of trouble when something untoward happened but, with a diesel, they just sat there listening to the engine roar and, if a warning light was illuminated, panic would set in. This was all in the early days of diesel. Mick and I would argue with the drivers about the efficiency and ease of the work on diesels compared to steam.

One driver, who was a resident in the hostel, Albert Banks, used to smoke a pipe with only half a stem and it was always stuck up against his nose. Another thing about old steam drivers was the size of their noses. I suppose looking out of a speeding loco all your working life with the wind buffeting your nose must do something to its looks.

Albert said that he could pick up speed with an old Lizzie as quickly as a new Class 40 diesel and one day he would prove it. The day came. He was on the mid-day Scot, Glasgow to London, and he would pick up the train at Carlisle Citadel station. It was arranged that he would blow his whistle on departure and we would time him going passed the shed. We would stop the clock, as it were, as the loco went under the footbridge. As Albert was a Carlisle driver and a right character, most of the shed staff knew him. About six of us apprentices were standing round the back of the shed by the ash plant, a road where the ash and clinker were unloaded from under the steam loco's ash pan. Someone noticed a man on the footbridge. He was dressed in a suit and bowler hat. We all thought he was a spotter as they get everywhere and the number of people getting numbers and taking photographs seemed to be growing, probably because steam was going to be phased out. We were all watching towards the station and counting the seconds after the whistle had gone. As the engine came into sight, it was really flying. Then the whistle sounded. We thought it was for our benefit but, as the train came towards us, we saw sparks coming off the wheels and brake blocks. As the loco was alongside us, the chap on the bridge jumped and the smoke box caught him in full flight. He was thrown to the side and the train slid by a couple of train lengths. We went over to him but could do nothing for him. He wasn't badly marked but every bone in his body was like jelly. He had folded his coat up neatly and placed his hat on the top of it before jumping. The train driver, Albert, and the guard walked back to us. Someone had telephoned the police and they soon arrived. Albert said he knew he was about to jump as soon as he saw him and made an emergency brake application but, to stop a train over five hundred tons travelling at speed takes a while and had no chance of stopping in time. Today, anyone involved with a fatality is taken off the footplate and interviewed by the police and an inspector and another driver takes the train on if the police allow it but I think the guard and Albert went back to the train and carried on to Crewe. No-one remembered to check the time.

Albert was diagrammed to work the Midday Scot regularly and this was the train I would catch sometimes on a Friday to travel back to Lancaster. It didn't stop at Lancaster but would thunder through and stop at Preston, then I would get a stopper back to Lancaster. This was quicker than going on the slow train from Carlisle that seemed to stop at every gate post.

Albert would invite me on to the footplate if he knew I was travelling and I would give the fireman a break and do a bit of firing. This was not really allowed and I had to keep out of sight going passed Penrith signal box. On one occasion, the mid-day Scot was running over half an hour late. I climbed in from the track side and Albert told me to drive. As soon as we had pulled away, I took the regulator and eased it fully open. Once we had the speed up I wound back the reverser very gently. This shortened the stroke of the valves, putting steam faster on to the piston heads. This created more speed and didn't use any more steam. I hid in the tender as we went through Penrith then took up the regulator again. We made very good time and as we went over the top of Shap I eased the regulator back because of a sixty m.p.h. caution going down towards Tebay and a sharp corner to Oxenholme. Albert grabbed the regulator and opened it up fully, "We are late lad, give it some stick", he shouted over the noise. I was sat on the driver's seat looking out of the left hand window, watching the track hurtling towards us. There is a speedo in the cab but I didn't have time to look at it because I couldn't take my eyes off the track. We went through Tebay so quickly that if I had blinked, I would have missed it. Then we took a sharp right hand curve towards Oxenholme. We hit that at a great speed and crabbed round. The belly plate, a strip of metal the width of the footplate and hinged on to the tender and about sixteen inches long which covers the join between loco and tender, was going from left to right and back again. If it had caught anybody's feet it would have had them over and probably damaged them as well. As we rounded the corner, I looked back and saw each carriage lurch into sight round the bend. They were rocking and swaying. I felt a great relief when the last one came into sight and all the train was still on the track. Someone must have informed the station master at Oxenholme because he was stood on the platform shaking his fist at us. Also, at Carnforth and Lancaster, station staff were waving and shouting but there was no chance of hearing anything at that speed. Albert took over when we were approaching Preston and we coasted to the end of the platform by the slope. We were on time, or almost. I climbed out on to the track, went round the front of the loco and up the slope to go to the adjoining platform for my train back to Lancaster. Coming along the platform towards the loco were irate station staff and the chef, in his white apron, brandishing a meat cleaver. It seems all the diners had been upset with the rocking and rolling of the buffet car and the food had gone everywhere. Albert ended up with three days' suspension. He didn't mind too much as we would both have ended up with the sack if anyone found out that I was driving and, as he said, "We made up time, they should be happy". For me, it was the most scary thing ever, even now I remember the feeling of trying to will the loco and coaches round that bend.

I soon got to go out with the breakdown as they already knew me from the tandem lifts they had done with Carnforth. As I was living in the hostel, just above the shed, I was a captive worker ready to go. I was quite often one of the first on the vans. The first job was to light the lamps as the riding van was gas lit . Then I had to stoke up the range to warm the water for the tea. When we got back into the shed from a job, everyone would bale out and go home except the foreman and the crane driver. The foreman had to finish his reports and the crane driver had to put his crane to bed and prepare for the next job. The fire had to be kept low and the water warm so steam could be brought up quickly. Because I lived so close I would get the job of gassing it up and filling the water tanks. The water was no problem but I never enjoyed gassing. Carlisle had its own gas plant and did it stink. A fitter and mate, two old boys worked there. The smell was in their skin and when they went out for a pint at night they would always be together in a corner. Everyone trying to avoid them because of the smell. When they retired no one would take up the job in the gas plant. Luckily, a new riding van arrived with batteries under slung and had a dynamo fitted.

The drop pit at Upperby was an old hydraulic one and would leak all the time so we would take the loco that wanted a pair of wheels removing round to Carlisle Canal shed as there was an electric drop pit there. The shed had been closed for a while but the workshop and drop pit were still usable, it was always a sign that the shed was going to close if major repairs were carried out or new plant installed.

One day, the N.U.R. had called a twenty four hour strike but, as apprentices, we were not allowed to go on strike so we were the only people in the shed with the foreman. He told us to sweep up and clean the workshop, then clear off. We did as he said. Most of us went swimming at the pool.

The strike started at midnight and any train that had started its journey had to continue. Even a train with a 23.59 departure time had to run. One of these late runners had arrived at Carlisle and the fireman, who lived at Penrith, was looking for a lift home. He had his bicycle with him but, as it was such a long way, he thought he would borrow a loco; an English Electric Class 40. I don't know how he got a key. They were like gold dust and only handed to a driver who was to work a train with a diesel and they had to be handed back on arrival at the shed. Because nothing was running and all the signal men were off, he thought he would be safe. He somehow got off the shed and was running down the main when he came to catch points. The loco was derailed and ended up on its side in a field. Seemingly, he was alright. He kicked out a window, got his bike out and rode off. He never came back again. The loco was well clear of the track but the railway wanted it recovered as soon as possible as it looked untidy to the passengers just lying there showing its wheels, traction motors and fuel tanks to the world. So it was arranged that we would depart 0030 the next day and meet Carnforth on site to re-rail it.

Though the capacity of the two cranes didn't come up to the weight of the loco, we had to do it and one good thing about steam was you just kept going. If the crane was bedded down properly and the load kept close to the floor, it was reasonably safe. We had to do a lot of digging to get under the flat side of the diesel to get the chains under it to right it. Also, we had to place timber between the chains and body-side to protect the new paint. As both gangs were experienced in using the cranes, if not re-righting and re-railing diesels, the job went well and we were soon on our way back to our respective sheds. It was nice seeing the Carnforth crew again and we did get a bit of time for a chat. I proudly told them of our new riding van with electric lighting but they had one too. It seemed that the breakdown vans were slowly being dragged into the 20th century.

As the steam was being phased out, companies were trying to come up with different forms of traction. One I liked the best was G.T. 3. This was a gas turbine loco on a Lizzie framing. I saw it one night on time trials and with thirteen sleepers on it, it just whistled away. It picked up speed even faster than a diesel. Another prototype was DP2. This was derailed just outside the shed, only one pair of wheels but, because it was a diesel, care had to be taken positioning the jacks. The one thing about a steam loco was that they were so robust and strongly built they could be jacked under any part of the framing without doing any damage.

The apprentices from Upperby would sometimes play football with the apprentices from Cowan Sheldons, the crane builders, and we found out that British Rail had ordered ten seventy five ton capacity breakdown cranes from them and they had started building the first. Big diesel locos weighed over one hundred tons, so on paper it was not possible to lift one with two of the original cranes. One dinnertime, I managed to go back into Cowans with the apprentices and see the new crane. The carriage was being assembled on an enormous jig and it was upside down with nothing to show that it would eventually be a crane. I found out its number was to be ADB 966111 and it was destined for Stratford, East London.

I thought how wonderful it would be to be in charge of a crane like that, never thinking that I would eventually get to Stratford as Breakdown Foreman, but that was to be in the future.

The shed at Carlisle, as I mentioned earlier, was a round house with a very deep turntable in the middle. The smoke baffles which ran above every road in the round house were so low they would be in the way of opening the roof doors. Because the roof doors would have had to be open in order to work on the engine of the diesels, they had to be worked on outside.

Unlike Carnforth, Carlisle had new electric hand lamps. They were so valuable that they had to be signed for out of the stores and returned to the stores at the end of every shift. We were given a large battery which fitted on a belt and a three foot cable which came out of the battery with the light on the end. It fitted our hands perfectly and had a clip to fit to a head band, like a miners lamp, in order to keep our hands free.

One day, a steam loco ran into the round house and the turntable was not set for it. It was at 90 degrees. The loco went straight into the turntable pit which was about five feet deep. The tender and rear pair of wheels were still on the track. Luckily, the table was crossways or it could have been damaged. Two locos in tandem were coupled to the tender to hold it and stop it moving forward whilst we jacked up the front. Using a crane was out of the question because of the roof and the only way into the shed was blocked by the incident. Because the rear wheels were on the track the loco pivoted round them as we lifted the front. Sleepers were used to pack up under the wheels and we soon had the front high enough to place rails, which had been previously cut to size, under the wheels. The rails were rolled over on to their sides and pushed up to the rails of the road on which the tender and two locos were standing. The loco was lowered on to the rails and the wheel flanges went into the side grooves of the rails. Then, by using the two locos to pull, the loco in the table came up and went straight on to the rails with only slight damage to the front end. All the lifting tackle was stowed away; the sleepers were put back in a wagon and another job successfully accomplished. I mentioned that it was lucky that the wheels went back on to the track but I was told that if it hadn't twisted it would go back the same way it had come off and I found this to be very true over the years.

The driver was not hurt and soon ended up in the office as an inspector. We said it was to keep him out of the way so that he wouldn't cause any more damage.

Carlisle was a much bigger shed than Carnforth with more staff; fitters, mates, electricians and boiler smiths. The boiler smiths ruled the roost and most of them were miserable. I was still spending more time working on steam than diesel and sometimes the fitter would tell me to get a boiler smith to do some cutting or warming. Their cabin was situated on one side of the round house and, when we went through the door, the heat would hit us. The boiler smith's who were not working on wash outs would be lazing around a pot bellied stove which was usually glowing a dull red with the heat and, if they were not asleep, they would be reading papers and not one of them would come straight away to help but always had excuses not to do anything. We would be told to clear off by the boiler smiths then get more abuse from the fitter when we went back and told him that one may turn up later. Mick and I thought, to get our own back on them, we would find some old rail detonators or fog signals (they are flat and round, sit on the top of the rail in groups of three at twenty foot intervals, are filled with an explosive powder such as gun powder, and are detonated when a loco travels over them making a very loud bang to alert the driver of the loco). We also had some shot gun cartridges. We climbed up on to the roof and dropped them down the chimney then made our escape by jumping on to the brick arch man's pile of sand. As we were flying through the air, two boiler smiths came round the corner just as the explosions started and realised what we had done and, as we were sprawled in the sand, they caught us. We both got a good hiding and we were thrown in the river which ran alongside the shed. As it was summer, the river was only about three feet deep but our revenge was sweet. The foreman knew what we had done but nothing was said. It was all part of working on the railway.

I was just sixteen when I went to Carlisle and had not been introduced to alcohol, and I didn't have enough money to go drinking anyway. However, two road learners from York would pester Mick and I to go out with them. We would reply that we couldn't afford it and they always said that, as they were loaded, they would pay. Eventually, we gave in and went out with them. The beer was ten pence a pint. We would start at the hilltop pub and work our way down Botchergate calling at all the pubs to the station then cross the road and work our way back finishing up at a fish and chip shop. We would go out with them as often as twice a week sometimes and meet lots of the fitting staff all in their favourite pubs. It seemed to me at that time that all railwaymen spent a great deal of their spare time drinking. This would prove to be the case all my railway career.

One winter morning, I was awakened by one of the hostel staff and was told that I was to go on the snow plough and my breakfast was ready. Quick as a flash, I was down in the dining room, finished my meal and off out expecting to see snow. It was five a.m. and a cold crisp night and all the stars were visible but no snow. I thought someone was having a joke at my expense but, as I arrived at the office, Tom, one of the breakdown fitters was there with a fitter's mate. We climbed up on the foot plate of a Lizzie that was fitted with a drift plough. We had a fifty ton hand jack and a sack with half inch bolts in it. The idea is that the plough is fitted to a framework and the framework is fitted to the front of the loco. On either side of the framework at the front is a half inch shearing bolt which holds the plough at the correct height and, to save any damage to plough or loco, these two bolts would shear and the plough would drop. The jack would be put under the front and the plough would be raised to match up to the holes for the bolts and off we would go again. The answer to my question of why we were going out on such a clear night was that the Station Master at Shap had seen a snowflake and rang Carlisle for a snow plough. As we approached Shap we saw that it was indeed snowing and was about two or three inches deep on the ground. Looking to the left and right all we saw was total desolation. The immediate mountains were more like black rolling hills, quite high but not rugged. We could just see the dry stone walls without a curve running straight over the high ground. The sky was very dark and full of snow. Apart from the station and a few cottages close to it the only buildings were stone built farms laying squat against the ground hiding from the vicious winds. A few small stone buildings or bothies stood by the track, they were permanent way cabins. We went over Shap summit down to Tebay and turned the loco on the turn-table to go over the down road. The next time we saw Shap, quite a while later, the snow was about two feet deep and a right blizzard was blowing. We cleared the down and went back to Upperby to couple another loco and plough at the back. We had nearly three hundred tons of locos and ploughs and off we went again on the up. Nothing else was running because of the snow because the line had blocked again soon after we had cleared it. We ran into the drifts time and time again and got over the summit. We then ran to Tebay and crossed over on to the down and charged at the snow blocking our path. We would set back and run at it again. We were changing shearing bolts every three or four times. The problem was that snow shifted from one line would block the other alongside. We, therefore, decided to concentrate on keeping just one line open. I think it was the down.

We returned to Carlisle and had another loco placed between the original Lizzies. Every time we went to Carlisle the footplate staff were changed but no one thought of relieving the poor fitting staff. We did more runs on the down road going wrong road south then back over Shap to clear track then wrong road again. Sometimes when the shearing bolts broke we were in such deep snow we had to dig our way off the footplate into a hole in the snow to the side and then the locos and ploughs would reverse away from us so we could then climb down to the track and work on the plough. After fitting the new bolts we would scramble into the hole we had dug and the locos would drive forward alongside us and we would climb on to the footplate. We thought we were winning but, as we were ploughing north, the snow was well above footplate level and it all collapsed behind us and even with three locos pushing we couldn't move it. To do any good we had to have a good run at the drifts. We were well and truly stuck. It was very embarrassing having the snow plough stuck in snow. The same as when the breakdown train derails. As there was nothing we could do we bailed out stepping over the telegraph wires that ran along side the track. We headed for the A6 as we could see lorry lights slowly negotiating the road. We crossed a field and, in the middle, we could see the grass. We managed to make the A6 and cadge a lift. We were running out of cigarettes. Luckily, the fitter's mate had got a carton of two hundred before we set off.

We weren't really dressed for snow. We had kept warm with working and on the footplate we were as warm as toast. We would warm our front then turn round and warm our backs. We were very cold trekking across the fields and the three of us had teeth chattering like castanets. We couldn't even speak. When the lorry stopped to pick us up all we could do was point in the direction he was going in and grunt at the driver. With four of us in the lorry cab and the heater going full blast we soon thawed out. We were dropped off on London Road just above the shed. The remainder of the cigarettes going with the driver as a thank you. We had been out twenty two hours, eaten nothing and only drunk what we could scrounge off the footplate staff. That same day a railcar on the Silloth line ran into a drift. It was the first train that morning and had only three or four passengers on board. They, with the driver and guard, walked back to the last station and got a bus. That line was left to the last to clear and the railcar, when recovered, was a total shambles. The anti-freeze had frozen in the engines and burst the blocks. Even though the driver and guard had shut all the doors and windows, the snow had got into the carriages and wrecked the seats and wall panels.

On the Saturday, most of the fitting staff who were not booked on were asked if they would help with a bit of digging and we would be paid ten shillings an hour. The idea was that we would leave Carlisle with a rake of Mermaids and load them up with the snow on Shap. We set off early Saturday morning to help the P way gangs. Two guards' brakes were on the back of the train full of railway men. We arrived and climbed out of the brakes and grabbed a shovel. I ended up with a quite large shovel and, after half an hour of digging, was worn out. A P way man half my size and three or four times my age gave me his smaller shovel and he used mine.

The Mermaids were side tipping ballast wagons, not very high sided but high enough as every shovel full was thrown above our heads into them. When all the wagons had been loaded the train went back to Carlisle and down the Settle line to tip the snow over the side of one of the viaducts and another rake of Mermaids was shunted into place. When this one had been filled I volunteered to go with it and tip the snow out.

It's a lot easier than digging and I was suffering with a bad back, arms and legs and any other muscles I had been using. I had never worked so hard in my life. After we had finished on the Saturday we were asked if we would do it all again on Sunday. As this was at double time, I again volunteered. It was a whole pound an hour. I managed to arrange to travel with one of the trains to do the tipping. Believe me, I wouldn't have been able to shovel all Sunday, even after a hot bath I could hardly walk.

With two hundred railwaymen digging from Carlisle and three hundred soldiers digging from the south nearly all the snow was removed, the locos and ploughs recovered and trains started running on the Monday. It was certainly a job well done and when pay day arrived I received twelve pounds for the twelve hour Sunday - three weeks wages in one day. It was almost worth the pain.

With all this new wealth I was able to go out drinking with the York drivers and stand my corner.

The ploughs were called out on a few occasions over Shap but we always managed to clear the roads without having to be rescued. Another place we had to plough was Beattock Summit to Carstairs. That was very bleak countryside which we had to plough through. I was getting used to pretty good money with all the overtime I was doing.

At least once a week the hostel would get a 'phone call to get me up early and they would have my breakfast ready and I would be picked up at the door by a fitter and mate in a railway van to go to Carlisle Citadel Station because a train was in trouble and we would have to put it right. Usually, it was an overnight sleeper losing amps or overheating coming up Shap but by the time it arrived at Carlisle the problem had usually rectified itself because it had coasted most of the way from the top of Shap.

There was a canteen on the station and we would adjourn to it for a second breakfast. The food was good and very cheap. Often we would be called by the public address system to go to another train in trouble. It could be a railcar or steamer and, once the drivers knew that fitting staff were in the vicinity, all the silly jobs like faulty light bulbs on the panel of railcars would require renewing or jubilee clips on water pipes would need tightening. There was also a back door to the Cumberland Hotel on the station which we would use. Some days we would spend the whole shift working on the station in the canteen or in the pub. As the public address system didn't work in the pub, we had to rely on station staff to inform us, but usually they would be in the pub first.

One day we had a royal train going through Carlisle and the loco was to be changed. We had two Class 40s cleaned and painted. One to go on the train and one as a stand by. Both locos had A exams and the first one left Upperby early and was ready to drop on the coaches as soon as the original one was released to the shed. As soon as the loco was coupled up the fireman started up the boiler for the heating in the train. Working on a royal train must have made him nervous because he flooded the boiler. The loco was taken off and the second one sent for and, would you believe, he did the same thing with that one. The original loco had arrived on the shed by this time and we had just finished refuelling it. I was told to stay with it and go back to the royal train and fire up the boiler. I would be let off at Preston.

The footplate staff and riding inspector were all in white shirts and ties and I was in overalls and clogs. I stayed in the engine compartment.

I had no problems with the boiler but the train was very late and the next day the press reported that the Queen didn't think much of diesels and would rather have her train pulled by a steam engine. How true their reporting was remained to be seen and in later life I realised that they would make up stories about incidents even when told what had happened.

At Christmas we had Christmas Day or New Year's Day off but not both. I had Christmas Day off at home. When I returned to Carlisle the breakdown gang had not been back at the shed very long. They had been called out early Christmas Day morning to an incident on the main line north of Penrith. It seems that on Christmas Eve some revellers had started an earth scraper and set it going. It was from the building of the M.6. It had travelled a good distance across the countryside taking everything in its path. The scoop was down and tons of soil and bricks were in the back. As it came to cross the railway it had to negotiate a cutting. The tractor unit hauled the scraper over the edge of the cutting down the bank and across the tracks but when it tried to climb the other side it was too steep an angle and came to rest blocking the up and down main lines with over one hundred tons of machine and dirt. I was told that when the gang arrived they cut the tractor unit from the scraper and lifted it back into the field. The scraper was more difficult because of its size and the weight inside, so they rolled it over emptying its load and then that went into the field as well. All the earth now blocking the tracks was removed by the permanent way gang. They had to put the track right anyway.

Because I had been off at Christmas, I was working the New Year and on New Year's Eve the apprentices found all the old detonators or fog signals and placed them on the ash plant track. There was over a hundred, about six inches apart ready for midnight and, as I lived so close, it was my job to run a loco over them at the stroke of midnight. We also tied string to the whistles of the locos in steam so that one man could set four or five off at the same time.

Some of the apprentices and young fitters had met me in the hill top pub and at a quarter to midnight we went down to the shed all knowing what we had to do to see the New Year in. It seemed a good idea at the time, as all silly ideas do over a pint.

I jumped on the shunting loco on the ash plant and had my transistor radio on to listen for Big Ben. At the stroke of midnight

I eased the loco forward over the detonators. I didn't hear any of the whistles because of the noise of the detonators going off. It was like a continuous explosion going on for ever. I stopped at the end of the road and got off the loco. I thought I was going to be deaf for the rest of my life. I met up with the other lads and it seemed to have been a success. We were well out of the way before the police arrived. They had so many 'phone calls that the shed was blowing up that they had to respond. It was about a week before I got my hearing back properly.

Another memorable and costly experience happened one day in the round house. I was talking to another apprentice. We were between two steam loco's having their boilers washed out and one of the electrical apprentices, Norman, was throwing coal at us from one of the footplates. As we were next to a three foot high water pipe (known as a swan neck because of its shape) connected to a wash out bag, I told the other apprentice to turn the water on as soon as I got hold of the nozzle end. He did and a good jet of water gushed out. I thought Norman had left the footplate and gone on to the framing on the other side. I aimed the jet of water over the boiler to catch him. I heard a shout and played the jet from end to end hoping to give him a good soaking but to my horror three bowler hats walked round the end of the loco, the Shed Master the Chief Clerk and Foreman. It did look so funny all three soaked with water dripping off their bowler hats. They didn't see the funny side of it and I got three days suspension.

I was soon to leave Carlisle. Most of the young fitters would go to work at one of the London sheds for a time to make some money after completing their six months loco erecting at Crewe then return to the north with enough for a deposit on a house. Although they weren't out of their time, they would be paid as journey men, only a few shillings lower than a fitter. This was because the London sheds were short of fitting staff.

Willesden

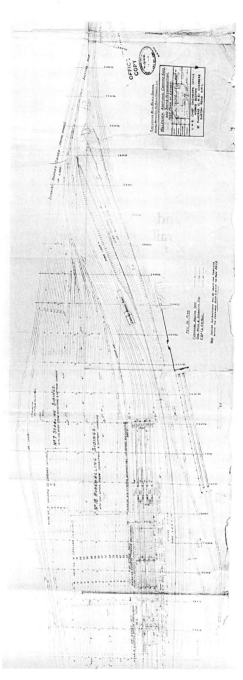

CHAPTER 3
MARYLEBONE 1

I decided to go to London before going to Crewe to do my compulsory works training and found a lovely little shed that only had diesel rail cars, Marylebone. My application to transfer was speedily dealt with but this time I arranged lodging before I left Carlisle. I was to live in the Hampden Club on Polygon Road off Eversholt Street by London Euston Station.

I arrived on a Sunday and booked into the hostel. This was purpose built for railway staff, mainly from Scotland and the North West, to lodge. As I had only the one bag to unpack, I soon settled into the lodgings and went to find Marylebone shed. I had been to London before with the school and so understood the underground system. I found the shed by asking railway staff at Marylebone station. It was only a short walk. The shed was situated between a block of flats and a dairy bottling plant. It was six roads wide and an eight car set would fit on each road. On the right was the old shed with three shallow pits and cobbled floors. It was an old carriage shed with a low roof and bad lighting. The three roads on the left had deep pits, very airy with strip lighting and loads of room between the pits to move between the D.M.Us.

We sometimes had to climb on the roof of D.M.Us at Carlisle, and clogs were forbidden on the roof. I asked the foreman if I would be allowed to wear clogs. I received a strange look and was told it was OK, and at no time would I be required to go on the roof.

The washing facilities were very good with white tiles everywhere and upstairs was the mess room, with tables and chairs and a couple of cookers and an urn for a continuous supply of hot water.

The foreman introduced me to a young Scottish fitter, Andrew Cruikshanks, who also lived at the Hampden Club and we arranged to meet at breakfast the next day. I met Andrew as

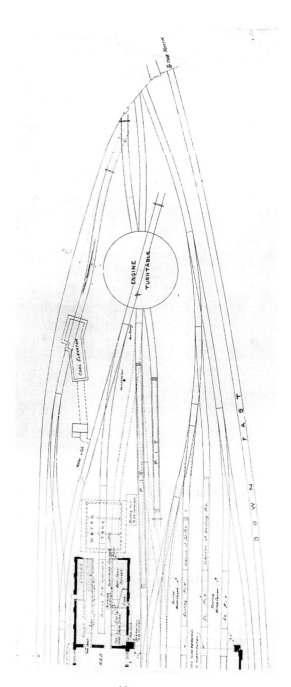

arranged and saw the food was the same as at Carlisle when I started there, swimming in fat.

We walked to King's Cross station and disappeared down a hole in the ground and on to the tube. As I got into the carriage I wished everyone a good morning as all northerners are brought up to do. A row of newspapers dropped about six inches under a row of eyes looking at me then went back up and not a word was said. Three stops later we alighted at Baker Street and Andrew explained that no one talks to anyone on the tube. I just thought they were all ignorant.

Now I realise they were all hoping I wasn't going to sit next to them in my overalls and clogs. Because I stood out in my clogs, I purchased a pair of boots from the Army and Navy Store and left the clogs at work.

Most of the fitting staff at Marylebone were foreign with just a few English, Irish or Scottish and one Welsh man. I was put to work with Andrew and was soon in the swing of things. Every lunch time we would adjourn to The Boston Arms or The Windsor Castle pub for lunch, and return two or three hours later and finish off that little bit we had left to do, then hand in the job sheets all signed up and go home or back to the hostel.

Most of the work was exams and was very repetitive. A monkey could have done it because there was no actual fitting at all.

One day we had an engine change and a store's wagon with a new engine was shunted into Number One road up to the buffer stops and behind it was a hand operated rail crane. The crane had a fixed jib and would not lift or lower, only the hook on the rope could be operated and this was by man power. A large wheel on either side of the rope drum had long handles sticking out and with three or four labourers on each side would turn the drum and lift the hook. The jib was slewed by turning the whole top of the crane again by hand.

The new engine was lifted out and placed on a pallet at the end of the shed. The crane and empty wagon were shunted out and the driving car put in its place. The engine which was to be replaced was then ready to be worked on. Everything was uncoupled except the actual mounting bolts. Once all the uncoupling was finished, two thin reinforced plates were put across the pit, then Andrew brought out an electric fork lift from a room close by. It stayed on charge when not in use and was locked up. He manoeuvred it on to the plates under the engine, then we put wooden packing across the forks which took the weight of the engine. The three mounting bolts were removed, and with a bit of manoeuvring we had the engine on the floor. Certain parts had to be transferred from the old engine to the new one. The fork lift was positioned under the new engine and put under the rail car, lifted up and the engine was secured by the mounting bolts. The fork lift and bridging plates were put back in the room and locked up. We coupled up the drive, water and fuel pipes and fan, then the electricians coupled it up electrically, which involved connecting four wires, and the engine was running before the end of the shift. The empty wagon and crane had to be shunted in when the rail car had been moved and all the labourers had to get back on the handles to load up the old engine.

Soon after my arrival at Marylebone a directive came out that apprentices would be required to move between the London sheds belonging to LMS. i.e., Camden, Willesden and Marylebone.

The first shed I was sent to was Camden. This was a round house and the loco's mainly steam. I did not enjoy this. The work was OK but the staff all knew their shed was to close soon and they were all as miserable as sin.

When I returned to my home depot on the Friday to pick up my wages I complained to the foreman that I had done all that kind of work before at Carlisle and I managed to get moved to Willesden. As a note of interest, Camden round house became a theatre, I certainly hope they cleaned it up first.

Willesden had a round house for steam and the diesels were worked on outside, the same as Carlisle. The staff were more friendly than at Camden, and a few lived at the Hampden Club, so I knew them.

With more apprentices we got up to more mischief and, as it was quite a big shed, the foreman was too busy to worry about the lads from other sheds, so we kept out of his way.

I would offer my services to fitters working on the diesels and picked up more information from them. At lunch time we would adjourn to the Fisherman's Arms or the B.R.S.A, (British Rail Staff Association) just outside the shed.

One of the chaps at Willesden was the blacksmith's striker. He was Polish and I couldn't pronounce his name, never mind spell it. His strength was phenomenal. He could lift up a driving wheel spring on his own and hold it in position for the fitter to put the holding pins in place. Without him we required two people lifting and two on bars to hold the spring up. Some of the bigger steam locos had nineteen or twenty leaves on each spring. If the leaves had broken or had been moved in the saddle with which they were held together, the spring had to be changed.

Firstly we had to take the weight off the spring with a hand jack and remove the retaining pins. As we were working in a dark pit with very little room everyone had to get out of the way when it dropped. At over two hundredweight it would easily break a leg or smash a foot.

Putting up the replacement spring was just as dangerous and many of the older fitters in steam sheds would have part of their index finger missing because, as they had been feeling if the hole in the spring and the hole in the spring hanger were in line, the spring had slipped and had chopped off half a finger. The younger lads would use a lolly stick or a pencil after seeing and hearing what could happen.

The Polish striker would, every evening after finishing work, stand naked in the blacksmith's bosh and have an all over wash, and cook his meals on the forge. He seemed to have no use for money because every three months he would be called into the office and made to pick up his wages, and we were all weekly paid. Some of us did explain about Building Societies, and we had to take him to one in Willesden and almost force him to join.

Another chap, who was a fitter's mate from the West Indies, would pick out six horses which were running that day and have a six horse accumulator bet. Nearly every day some of them would win but not all and he won nothing. We, the young lads, would explain about doubles and trebles, but he would do just the one bet. He would tell us what he had picked and we would bet on them in doubles and trebles and we made a handsome profit.

One day I was working with a fitter on an English Electric Class 40 and the oil sample we had taken out of the sump was contaminated with coolant. This indicated that the liners were leaking. The liner is a large steel tube about three foot long and a foot across. It is fitted in the engine block with the cylinder head bolted on top. The piston travels up and down in it. We found three liners leaking and removed them. The lips round the top of all three had small cracks and holes pitted in them. This lip sits on the block and must be very smooth. The only way to save a liner like that, if possible, is to hand grind it.

A sleeper was put across a pit and the upturned liner placed in the middle of it. The grinding ring was placed over this and, with a couple of dabs of grinding paste between the faces, we started twisting the grinding wheel to left and right. After an hour our arms were so tired they felt as if they were going to fall off. We lifted the ring off and cleaned the old paste off the face and examined it, and finding very little change we started all over again. Sometimes a small hole gets bigger and we knew we had a lot more grinding to do. It took three days to get them acceptable to the foreman. As I had told everyone that I was a diesel apprentice, I was lumbered with most of the grinding.

About this time a new shed was being built at the other side of the main road and I was told to take some lubricating oil and fill one of the lubricators on a Class 40 that was standing in the new shed. I went over and was amazed at what I saw. This brand-new shed was all concrete and glass with tiled pits and red and green anti slip paint on the floor. I topped up the lubricator which was on the left of the drivers' steps and spilled some oil on the floor, not very much, and I thought nothing about it. That afternoon the main man at Willesden saw the oil and made enquiries about who had been in there. I was called to his office, given a dressing down, and told to clean it up.

I managed to get on to the breakdown gang in the day time only and, as there were lots of yards in the area, I was often out with them re-railing. The most usual vehicles to derail were ten foot wheelbase coal wagons. One day at about 0800 we got a call to the main line outside Euston. An empty passenger train was being propelled from the carriage sidings into Euston and took the wrong road and hit a Class 31 waiting at a signal. The driver and fireman or second man saw the train take the wrong road and tried to get out. The second man jumped out on to the track but the driver must have slipped and, as the train impacted on to the front of the thirty one, it pushed the driver's desk against a large fire bottle which stood about five feet high against the back bulk head of the cab and trapped the driver. When we arrived, the ambulance and firemen were already there. The medics had a line into the driver's top half and he was talking. The main man at Willesden was there and wanted to try and get him out gently but the fire chief wanted the front of the cab pulled away as quickly as possible to get the driver to hospital. As the top fireman was always in charge of train accidents, his instructions had to be adhered to. As the front was pulled away by another loco, the driver fell in two.

The film industry seemed to like using railway settings for films. They were filming part of 'The Ipcress File' in a wagon sheet shed at Willesden. They were there all day. The old doors were removed. These were high double doors and very heavy. New ones made out of balsa wood were put up in their place. A few of us were watching and managed to get a dinner from the caravan dishing out food. They filmed a Land Rover hurtling along in front of some railway cottages. It swung round through the gate, then crashed through the balsa wood doors. We, the railway staff, were asked to keep out of shot so we stood behind a wagon. Our legs can be seen on the film for a split second below the sole bar. Marylebone Station was often used for filming people departing and arriving. Clive of India and the Beatles 'Hard Days Night' were just two of them. 'The Day of the Triffids' train crash was filmed there. It was all done very slowly with a big fan behind the buffer stops. As the steam train approached the stops with lots of steam and smoke being blown back over the loco, it looked as if it was travelling at great speed and, when the loco buffered up to the stops, the driver opened the cylinder cocks at the bottom of the steam chest and on the speeded up film it seemed to blow up.

Harry Worth did some filming at the back of Marylebone shed one Sunday at the washing plant. He was supposed to have been left on the train asleep and, when he awoke, he opened the window just as his coach was being washed. The flails had been disconnected and only the water jets were working to safeguard him from being hurt.

A couple of years later, the main washing plant at Marylebone was scrapped and new lightweight washers were erected at the end of each road coming from the new shed. The idea was that every train departing from the new shed would be cleaned automatically and would not have to be shunted over to the washing plant just for this. As the track for one and two roads came out of the shed they curved towards three road which was almost straight out. The people who put the lightweight washers up hadn't allowed for the curve and both washers on one and two roads were demolished by the first trains which went through them. This was an expensive learning exercise in train gauging.

I occasionally worked with the breakdown gang at Marylebone and as they had very little equipment and didn't get many callouts there was no regular gang. The breakdown train was one van with messing and storage space pulled by a rail car driving coach at each end. Any jobs bigger than a wagon or one bogie off would be covered by Willesden.

One day I was walking along one of the platforms of the station. It was early afternoon and a unit was approaching. I stood back on the platform away from the opening doors. Railway men and passengers have been badly injured by being struck by doors opened early by impatient passengers. The driver started blowing the horn and shouted to me as he went past. I couldn't understand what he was saying but, as the unit passed me, I could hear the wheels sliding on the rails. The unit had picked its wheels up. This is the term used when all the brakes are locked on. It collided with the buffer stops at about five miles per hour and some of the passengers were thrown out of the open doors. I went back to check that the driver was alright and he was, but shaken up. We both then went to see to the passengers. The ones who had fallen on to the platform were all getting up complaining noisily, so they were O.K. One chap had lost a shoe. It had gone down between the platform and the train. I squeezed myself between the gap and retrieved it for him. It was still as good as new.

One of the station staff had dialled 999 and called an ambulance. It was then that we found an old chap had gone head first between the back of a seat and its cushions.

The cushions are held in place by two rubber clips and easy to release. We soon removed the seat cushion and lifted the old chap out so that the ambulance men could see to him, but it seems he had suffered a heart attack and they couldn't do anything for him. I thought he was the only one injured, but later at an enquiry I was told fifty people had put in claims for personal injury, ripped suits, damaged shoes, broken watches and spectacles and lost briefcases, all very expensive. I thought this strange as there were only fifteen people on the train. When I queried the number I was told that all the claims would be met as the railway didn't want to get any bad publicity.

CHAPTER 4
CREWE

As I mentioned earlier, all Midland apprentices had to do six months loco erecting at the main works, and I was sent to Crewe. I vacated my room in the Hampden Club and set off one Monday morning.

I met a couple of apprentices from Willesden on the train and they were always up for a laugh, so I thought it may be a good six months. On arrival at Crewe we went to the main offices and booked in. We were given addresses of places that may take borders for the six months and these were all in different areas of Crewe so we got split up straight away.

I ended up on Nelson street and a nice old lady offered me a room but told me her husband was dying from cancer and was sometimes noisy at night. As he was downstairs in the front room and my room would be upstairs at the back, I took it. Two other lads lodged with her. They were on the signal and telegraph side and in all the six months I never saw them go out. They either sat in front of the television or were studying.

Crewe Works was massive, almost seven miles long. I had been told which bus to catch and what gate to go in and on Tuesday morning I joined the throng. It was in February '63 and thousands of people worked there. Fleets of buses made there way to different gates of the works and would be waiting in long lines at the end of the shift to take the staff home again in the evening.

The main work in Crewe, besides the railway, was Rolls Royce and Cadbury's chocolate factory.

I was put to work with a group of fitters working on steam loco frames. I was to run copper pipe for the lubricators and grease lines. I found this boring, though the chaps who worked there seemed a friendly bunch and most of them had worked together for a while.

My job was boring but not as bad as one fitter's who, all day, would run a die nut down the horn stay bolts. When I asked him how long he had been doing that his reply was, "Over twenty years". At the time I thought he must be brain dead.

If we were more than a quarter of an hour late for work in the morning, we would find the gates locked and not start work until after the lunch break. We, therefore, would lose half a day's pay. This seemed a Draconian rule, but all of them were. We had a fifteen minute break in the morning and no break at all in the afternoon. In the morning break, tea ladies with their trolleys would position themselves in their allotted spaces and, if we fancied anything on the trolley, we had to get to the front of the queue before everything was sold out. Cheshire cheese sandwiches with onion were the most popular, and everyone enjoyed a sticky bun. Because there was no break in the afternoon, the local fitters would ask one of the shed apprentices to take their brew cans to the urns dotted about and fill them up, as the locals were too scared to do this and may get caught. We had the cheek and would do it for them. The brew cans would disappear into the fitters' tool lockers and we would see a fitter with one hand on the door almost climb in to drink a cup of tea out of sight of the charge hand.

Every ten fitters had a charge hand who operated from a four foot by four foot cabin. Inside was a high stool and a narrow shelf for a desk. One morning, to show how threatened the fitters were we, the shed apprentices working on the framings, were reading the papers we had bought on our way to work and the charge hand came out of his little cabin and clapped his hands. All the local fitting staff started to work and we carried on reading. He came over to us and said, "Now lads I've clapped my hands" and, as one, the six of us all gave him an ovation. The next day I was moved from there to the weigh bridge. Again, it was steam engines that I was working on. The weigh bridge was in its own building which was just long enough for a loco. The track was in six foot sections and had a weight gauge fitted to each section.

This would show the weight on each wheel. By pulling down on the spring hanger bolts the weight would alter and we could balance the locos. About ten fitters and mates worked there and had the work off to a fine art. The spanner to adjust the weight was long enough for four men to push and a rope on the free end long enough for the others to pull. This was hard and heavy work. I think it was a penance for cheeking the first charge hand. I didn't enjoy my time in there but later, when I had a crane that repeatedly broke springs and hanger bolts, I knew how to balance it and stop it breaking the springs.

I soon got out of there and managed to get into the brass shop. The main work there was re-building steam injectors and re-shaping bearings that had been slightly damaged. It was very quiet in there and there was not a lot of work to do. I started a small business of my own manufacturing diesel loco starting keys and selling them to the drivers and fireman for five shillings each. Making poker and toasting fork handles was another little perk. I cut one and a half inch squares of flat copper, aluminium, brass and red and green plastic out of the old oil lamps. I would then drill and tap a thread down the middle and tighten them on to a bar. The metal and plastic could then be worked on in a lathe and I would make lovely handles. I also made little brass buckets about two inches high with wire handles. I managed to use most of the machines in the brass shop for my own purposes. I found an old smock in one of the lockers and a clip board. After setting up my machines and getting them working I found I could wander round the works dressed in the smock and looking at the clip board and see my friends without being challenged. All the people I walked passed in my wanderings would avert their eyes and pretend that they hadn't seen me.

After a few weeks I was moved to nine shop, the main erecting shop. It must have been almost half a mile long. They were still re-building steam locos in nine shop, as well as diesels and I managed to get to work on building new Class 47s.

The workshop had a very high glass roof and was noisy. Overhead cranes straddled the five or six roads and ran the full length of the shop. It seemed that most of the work force at Crewe were employed in that shop, also ten shop next to it. The noise from the air operated tools could be very loud and, with the hundreds of people trying to shout to each other over the noise, it was deafening.

Outside at the north end of the shop was a traversing table that went all the way across the front of the two workshops. If a loco was ready to come out of the shop, it would be lifted by two of the big cranes and placed on the track by the doors. The table would be set with its rails in line with the road the loco was coming off and held in position with two locking pins. A hauling rope would be fastened to the loco from an electric capstan on the table. The capstan would then slowly haul the loco out of the shop and pull it onto the table. Once the loco was on the middle of the table the wheels would be scotched to keep it secure. The table would then be gently traversed along rails it ran on, carrying the loco to another track. With the table in position, end on to the track which the loco was to go on to, the securing pins would be locked into position and a shunting loco would run on to the table and be coupled to the new or rebuilt loco and haul it away to the next workshop for further work.

My job was fitting the body sides. Each side had two sections with holes already cut for door, windows and foot steps which had to be measured and cut to size with a windy nibbler. This was an air operated tool that chewed or nibbled at the edge of the metal and, with a bit of practice, I could get a good edge. When we were measuring the two bits we had to make sure the holes for the windows, door and foot steps were in the right place. Also, there was a hole for the boiler water which was ten inches in size and would eventually have a flap put on the inside into which a hose pipe or the big bag from a water crane could be placed to fill the boiler water tank. After boilers were removed and electric train heating introduced these were redundant and blanked off.

The two sections were placed edge to edge on a sixty foot table and secured with clamps and wedges. Then, a welder would tack weld down the join. After this I would turn the whole side over with the help of a five ton overhead crane and then the welder would run a weld along the full length of the join. It was turned over again for the final run of weld on the tacked side, then I had to grind it smooth with a windy grinder. I wore goggles for this, similar to a divers' mask, with one window in it. That summer it was so hot the sweat would build up inside the mask and my cheeks were awash. I had to keep pulling the mask away from my face to let the sweat run out.

Because of the heat, all the roof glass was white washed to stop the sun's rays from coming into the shop. We were told the chocolate factory stopped work and the staff were sent home because the chocolate wouldn't set.

Working with an electric welder, I was always getting arc eyes. The first time it happened I was watching the welder strike up and flash, I was blinded for a moment. I thought nothing of it until that night in bed when my eyes felt as though they had burning sand in them. The next morning I went into work with very red eyes and the charge hand sent me to the work's hospital.

The hospital was quite modern with a doctor and nurses. It wasn't for in-patients but they dealt with all kinds of accidents every day. I was soon looked at and given some Golden Eye ointment in a little tube and told to be more careful in future.

Back to the body sides. After I had completed cleaning up the weld, the body side was ready to go on the loco frame. I would whistle up a five ton crane and the crane driver would whiz up to my end of the shop, pick up the body side and we would offer it up for the welder to tack it in to place. Once it was in position, I would leave the welder to his job and take the crane and start on the next two pieces for the other side. When both sides were on they had to be tightened. This was done by a welder with a gas gun heating the body side between the struts it was welded to. The welder would warm up one small bit from the inside and I was on a trestle on the outside with a water spray cooling it down. Different welders would make different patterns to ease the boredom, and this tightened the body side skins.

One day a loco was being got ready to be lifted off its bogies next to where we were working. I had got down from the trestle to fill the water container at a tap further down the shop. As I was there, there was a bang and a lot of shouting by my loco. I rushed back and saw the loco which had been lifted was flat against the loco I was working on and the trestle was a mound of crushed scrap. I hadn't told the welder I was going to get more water and he thought I was crushed between the sides of the two locos. The two cranes lifting the finished loco were not central over the load and, as they took a lift, the loco went up and across to the next road which we were working on. Apart from the welder being knocked over and the trestle getting crushed, no damage was done to the locos but both crane drivers received their marching orders.

At least once a week a large party of train spotters would come round the erecting shop, and it was surprising the different types of people who were interested in the building of loco's. I would think there were almost as many women and girls as there were men.

In nine shops there were cranes of different capacity. The fifty ton cranes worked in two's and these were closest to the roof. Beneath the fifty tonners were the twenty ton cranes and below them the five ton cranes. As the shop was very long many cranes were needed. If I remember correctly, there were ten of the fifty ton cranes and about twenty five of the five ton cranes. I don't remember how many twenty ton cranes there were.

When two of the big cranes were traversing down the shop with a steam loco or diesel the smaller ones had to move in front of them so as not to impede them. One day a steam loco was being brought into the shop with two of the fifty tonners and one of the smaller ones ran into the lifting equipment suspended from the hook of the first fifty ton crane. With an almighty crash the loco fell to the floor and muck and dust showered down from the cranes. This happened above the area where the bogies were being worked on. All the bogies were on stands, one at each corner, about two foot high. None of them had wheels in position and all of them straddled the pit. They were about a foot apart with a pit board between them so we could walk between the bogies from one side to the other. When the falling steam loco hit them they toppled like dominos falling, about twenty altogether and very many fitters were injured.

Crewe was very security conscious or, at least, they gave that impression. One day when I was in the erecting shop a lorry arrived at the main gate with a single driver. I suppose he had some sort of paperwork with him, because he asked for some labourers to help him load up. Four labourers were instructed to help him and jumped on the back of the lorry. The lorry stopped behind the brass shop stores and was loaded up with bearings and brasses for locos and wagons. With a few tons of brass on board, the lorry went back to the main gate and away, never to be seen again. The lorry driver had given each labourer five shillings for helping him. It seems that's all it cost him for a lorry load of brass. The main gate security were very embarrassed.

One of the entrances to the works was over Eagle Bridge, close to the foundry. I used to look in there as I passed by and it always looked very dark and noisy. I was told that all the staff in the foundry were given two pints of milk per day because of the heat. After the shift had finished more pints would be consumed and it wasn't milk. I remember the white sand which was used for making the moulds. It was so fine it was like powder.

I had some friends in one of the machine shops and, if the work was slack, I would drop in for a chat. The most impressive machine was a new shaper. It could machine multiple bogies at one setting up. It was over thirty yards long and had only the one operator. I was told that, when it was installed, the tolerances were within one millimetre. Other machines would mill, then drill, turn the work over and work on a different side. This was all done with a tape instructing the machine. The tape was similar to that in a tape cassette.

There were also rows of pattern lathes. A pattern would be fixed to the front of the lathe and a carbon rod, not unlike a pencil, would run along the pattern. The cutting tool would cut into the metal spinning in the lathe and make a perfect profile of the pattern. It seemed to me that machining was getting easier.

Marylebone

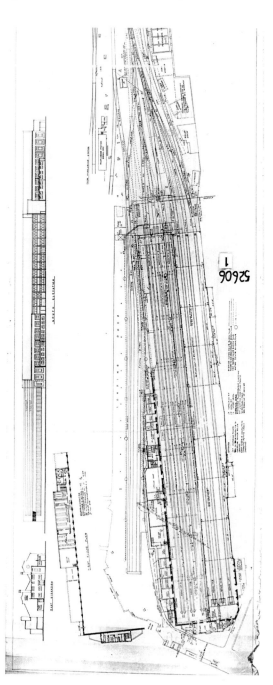

CHAPTER 5

MARYLEBONE II

After my six months was up I returned to Marylebone and the Hampden Club. I even got my old room back.

Although I was still only eighteen, I persuaded the foreman to make me up to a journeyman and because of the shortage of fitters this was accepted. I was working on exams and component changes on the B.U.T railcars. It was all so easy and the work was not too heavy.

One of the regular jobs was changing cylinder head gaskets. Firstly the coolant was pumped out into a tank so that it could be reused, as blue anti freeze was expensive. After removing the rocker covers, the inlet and exhaust pipes were taken down. Because the engines were horizontal we would get a seat to sit in front of the engine. After the rockers, injectors and fuel pipes were out of the way, we could undo the cylinder head nuts with a torque spanner.

Each head would cover three pistons and, if the gasket had been blowing between the piston cylinders, carbon would be blown up the cylinder head studs. This made it awkward to remove and sometimes easing oil would have to be squirted down the studs to soften the carbon. Once the head was on the floor, the two faces on the head and the block had to be scraped clean of the old gasket.

The gaskets were laminated copper, asbestos and aluminium, and had to be treated carefully to make sure they didn't bend or kink whilst being replaced. The head was then placed on the studs and the nuts were tightened in sequence and everything was put back, finishing with the coolant. (An interesting point is that, when setting the tappets after refitting the rocker arms, the engine oil dipstick was 20 millimetres thick. This was the setting for the tappets, and instead of looking through the tool box for the feeler gages, everyone would pull out the dipstick and use that.)

A cylinder head gasket change would take a shift to complete but that included a couple of hours in the Boston Arms or Windsor Castle. One night Andrew Cruikshank and I had one to change in a hurry for the morning service and the coolant was still hot as we replaced it. We changed the gasket in under an hour.

As I was working as a fitter, I had my own tools and a tool locker to keep them in. It was made of wood and was about three feet high, two and a half feet wide and the same in depth. The fitters would stick posters or flags of their country of origin on the doors.

Being a bit of an artist I would go one better. I ground a hacksaw blade into a sharp knife and carved into the bottom half of the door the Union Jack. Then with small pots of paint used by model makers bought from Beatties, I painted it. It was my pride, the best looking locker in the workshop. One of the other lads, Bobby Lake, was an avid Leighton Orient supporter and he asked me to carve and paint the Orient logo on his cupboard, which I did and he was more than pleased. Because the wood was soft and easy to carve, I made my own coat of arms above the Union Jack. With rampant lions, crowns and steam locos, everyone thought it good except the foreman who asked if I didn't have enough work to do.

All the fitters would alter some of their spanners to fit certain jobs. The exhaust manifold nuts were very awkward along the back of the manifold and everyone would have a bent ring spanner which would fit round the back. Some of the open jaw spanners would be ground down very thinly to fit tight spaces.

The traction at Marylebone was mainly diesel rail cars but we did have loco hauled trains with vans departing from the station, and sometimes we would be required to carry out running repairs.

One of the younger drivers was setting back his train into a shed at Great Missenden and, as the loco went into the shed, the door on the driver's side of the shed was caught by a gust of wind and swung towards the loco. The driver was leaning out of the window watching his train back. The driver had no time to stop or get out of the way and was decapitated. On examination it was found that the wood at the bottom of the door was rotten and, the bolt into the floor that held the door open was pulled away from the wood.

I mentioned earlier about the hand operated crane. That became obsolete when a new column crane was installed by the buffer stops on one road. It was a pillar about eighteen feet high with a rotating boom on the top, and an electric winch for lifting and lowering, very modern. The old crane was shunted over to the milk dock at the back of the shed next to the dairy bottling plant.

We used to drink with the dairy lads in the Boston Arms and quite often they would tell us a mistake had been made on the sell by date of their produce and were unable to distribute their goods so we could have them. There would be single and double cream, cottage cheese with different flavours and yoghurts of all kinds. After eating so much yoghurt I went off it for many years.

A new foreman arrived and ran the shed from the Windsor Castle public house. He decided the old crane should be scrapped, and the crew who worked on the breakdown would do the cutting up because we used gas cutting torches and we would do the work on weekends. We had to cut it up into manageable pieces to load on a lorry. We did well out of the weekend work but used an awful amount of gas.

Sitting in the Windsor Castle one afternoon, I brought up the amount of scrap which was going every Sunday night, about four lorry loads by then. I asked what was happening to the money. The foreman said we had done well out of the Saturdays and Sundays but he would supply us all with new tools. Once the crane was dispatched in small sections we looked for more scrap. Rails, chairs, the old washing plant, everything metal was put to the torch. Another couple of weekends gained, which meant more money in the wage packet.

About two months later the foreman kept his promise and we all had new tool boxes with bright shiny spanners.

On a Friday afternoon we would often wander down Church Street to check out the market and shops. There was a large estate just off Church Street and people were moving out in preparation for the redevelopment of the area.

One day I had gone over to the Barge Sidings with a fitter's mate to check a unit. The siding ran alongside the Grand Union Canal and that's how it got its name. As we examined the unit there was a bang and a manhole cover shot in the air about fifty feet away. We thought it was a bomb, then there was another bang and, again, a manhole cover flew into the air. So, giving the covers a wide berth we returned to the shed to report the strange goings on. It seems that the drains from the estate ran under the Barge Sidings and, because no toilets were being flushed, there was a build up of gas and, in the hot weather, it ignited causing the explosions.

The breakdown was occasionally called out to minor derailments, and one Sunday in June '65 I was called into work to go with the gang to Neasden. A guards brake had split the points and, when we arrived, was derailed both axles. The rest of the train had been uncoupled and put to one side. The gang consisted of me and three others.

When re-railing a vehicle which is off both axles the nearest pair of wheels are always put onto the track first. This is so that the vehicle will swivel on the rails and not dig into the dirt.

We had an old traversing jack which was very heavy. The base was a cast steel frame thirty inches long and twelve inches wide. On the top of this was a saddle that sat on slides either side of the frame and on the saddle was a jack. A thick screw ran the length of the frame and through the saddle. The idea was that the screw was wound so that the saddle was at one end, the frame was then positioned on wooden packing with the jack central to the lifting point, normally the middle of the buffer beam and, after placing blocks of wood between the bottom of the axle boxes and horn stay straps, this would stop the wheels dropping down as the body was lifted. The vehicle would then be jacked up one end only. Wooden scotches had to be placed under the wheels at the other end to keep the vehicle stable, and prevent it from moving forward or backwards. The only movement wanted was lateral. Once the wheels were clear of the ground the screw would be turned and the saddle would move with the jack on top of it and the whole vehicle would inch across towards the rails. I had learned never to lift anything too high, just to clear the ground. When the wheels were almost touching the rails and, if there was enough screw left to position the wheels over the rails, it would be jacked up clear then screwed the four inches to get the wheels in position then the jack was lowered and that was one pair of wheels re-railed.

The lifting equipment and wooden packing would then be carried to the other end and the whole process would start again. Firstly the axle boxes would be blocked and scotches placed under the re-railed wheels.

The wooden packing on the Marylebone breakdown train was not very good. Most of it was split or damaged and the gang had to build up a good bed with what was available. A busy gang would have tons of packing, all hard wood. Different gangs would have their packing cut to different lengths. Packing was from one inch up to six inches thick, Marylebone had packing of eighteen inches long and a foot wide. Some gangs, usually the ones with a crane, had packing three feet long and eighteen inches wide to use when packing under the outriggers.

Once we had completed the re-railing everything was cleared away onto the train and the re-railed vehicle was examined.

On this particular day a piece of wood was stuck between the point's blade and the rail. I had a six feet long crowbar and eased them apart so the wood could be recovered. Just as it was lifted out the bar slipped and it caught my head right on my hair line in the middle. What I thought was sweat, was blood pouring down my face.

I was taken to Willesden General Hospital and given the once over. After I was stitched and bandaged, the doctor wanted to admit me for observation, because it was a head wound. I didn't want to stay in hospital all night and I knew that I could sign myself out. I asked about this and was given a disclaimer form, and I left. The reason I remember the date so well was that it was the first day back at work after my honeymoon, and I didn't want anyone ringing my new wife telling her I was in hospital. I was fit for my next shift.

Marylebone had a high risk area for fatalities which was alongside Napsbury Mental Hospital. Some of the patients were fascinated by the railway and would wander onto the track.

Once, on a derailment by the hospital grounds, we were questioned by some of the patients over the fence. They knew more than us about the running of the trains, the times, and destinations.

I was asked to work at Aylesbury for two weeks in the summer period as the resident fitter was going on annual leave and it would be two weeks of nights. All I had to do was get the units running for the morning service and maybe top up a few radiators. I went up to Aylesbury on the Sunday night getting the last train out of Marylebone. On arrival I went to the station master's office, and was told that all the staff were in the B.R.S.A. club. It was getting better by the minute. As I always carried my B.R.S.A. card with me I went and joined in with a party that was going on. I saw the station staff and went to talk with them. They were the only ones in uniform and they told me everything was sorted and that there was nothing to do until four o'clock in the morning when the first units were to be started. The party went on well into the morning, then we all went into the office for tea. When it got to four o'clock I said I would start up the first units to go out and was told to take it easy as one of the station staff was doing it, and if he had any trouble he would call me.

I thought about asking when the resident fitter would retire and I would like to apply for this post but he wasn't that old and stayed there well after I had moved on from Marylebone. I did enjoy my two weeks though. I went back to Aylesbury quite a few times after that fortnight.

The winter months were totally different. With the drop in temperature the batteries would lose their charge and starting the railcars was very difficult. Sunday nights were the worst because the units had been shut down all weekend. I would try all sorts of tricks, even lighting a fire under the engines to warm the oil.

Diesel multiple units ran singly and in pairs and, occasionally, three would be coupled together for Nottingham trips. Each unit was made up of two power cars and two trailer cars. The power cars had two engines under slung, and a small driving cab at one end. These would be positioned at either end of a pair of trailer cars enabling the driver to drive from either end.

On the cold winter nights at Aylesbury, especially on Sunday, six units were on charge and should start. Once I had them running I put other units on charge and gave their batteries a boost. I didn't have time to put all of them on charge and sometimes, if three engines were running, I would get a driver to move the unit along in gear and I would run alongside trying to start the fourth. Having the unit moving took strain off the engine starter motor and more often than not worked.

The resident fitter at Aylesbury suffered with piles and this problem always got worse in the winter months.

One of the car accessory firms brought out an easy start aerosol spray and one blast in the air filter on a car would usually do the trick. I purchased a can and tried it out on a stubborn engine one night. As the air filter for the engine was an enclosed oil bath and about three feet from the inlet ports, I had to remove a plate on the inlet manifold and spray in there. As long as the starter motor would turn the engine it usually worked. Sometimes I would remove the rocker covers and decompress the valves. Without compression, the engine would rotate more easily. I would give a quick squirt with the easy start then gently put the compression on the engine with it turning. This would get the most stubborn engines going, but it all took time and I used a tin of easy start in one night. It was going to be expensive, so I asked if we could have it in the stores. I was told we couldn't as it would all be taken home.

One night I arrived at Aylesbury and the weather was good. I was looking forward to going into the B.R.S.A. club. I went to the station master's office and walked into an incident. The office was full of police and station staff. Apparently, someone had pulled down the signal wires North of the station. This seemingly was a common occurrence. A rope would be thrown over the wires and tied to the back of a van and the wires would be pulled down. The railway had fitted an alarm to this stretch of wires and that night, as I was arriving, it had gone off. The police and railway staff would ride in a rail car along the single line. The train would be in darkness with no lights at the front or in the carriages. I was asked to join in. The unit which was the nearest to the branch line was in good repair with no exhaust blows on the engines. Because the police wanted to ride along the track as quietly as possible an exhaust blow would shatter the silence. I climbed in with the driver and station master who was on the second man's seat. I sat on the desk next to the hand brake. With just the two rear engines running, again for quietness, we set off. One of the police officers was shining a small torch on the wires to let us know when we had arrived at the damaged area. I was leaning back with my face turned to the windscreen looking forward into the black night. Suddenly I saw some cows on the track. I shouted to stop but it was too late, and even at the slow speed we were travelling, we couldn't stop. Out of the six cows three were killed or had to be destroyed by a vet. It seems that the vandals who had stolen the wire had knocked down a fence and they had herded the cows onto the track. They used the cows on the track to give them plenty of time to load up the wire and make their getaway. We believe the same group was caught a month later but wouldn't admit to stealing the wire previously or putting cattle on the railway.

I found that changing shift every week didn't go well with my internal clock, and I would take days to adjust to a new shift. Therefore, I went onto regular nights and met others who didn't like days.

I soon became the darts' captain of the Windsor Castle and kept a set of tools behind the bar. I also had tools behind the bar in the Boston Arms. The train Crew Supervisor would call the pub if a unit or loco was in trouble at the station. The landlady would take the call and then hand me my tools and relay the message to me. I would run to the station as there never was very much time. The drivers of the units usually arrived about five minutes before departure time and, if anything was wrong with the train, started screaming for a fitter.

We had a newspaper train which would depart Marylebone early in the morning for the Midlands. One of the carriage and wagon staff would every night go down to the station and bring back armfuls of papers, and sometimes he would give me one. He told me his boy had a paper round and he would supply the papers. I don't know what his customers thought because they were all Midland papers, and all the television programmes were different to London's.

One night I was called to the station to check a unit low on coolant. With a watering can at the ready, I went across the milk dock and down an eight foot wall via a metal ladder set in the brick work. A unit was coming out of the station on the track which was close to the wall. I didn't see or hear it until it was almost on top of me and I dived to the ground and tried to press myself into the wall. I lay there trying to make myself as small as possible and hoped the jacket I was wearing wouldn't get caught by any of the running gear. As it was dark the driver didn't see me. After the train had passed I found the watering can down the track had been buckled. I spoke to the driver later and told him he nearly had me and he was more upset than I was.

On the 9th June, '67, I was called home off nights as my wife was thought to be going into labour. It was about three o'clock in the morning and I arrived home in record time only to be met at the door by my wife saying, "Its O.K., its stopped". I did take her in later that morning and at 1925 hours I became a dad for the first time. After seeing my wife and baby girl Gillian were fine, I went to work. There was no time off for new fathers.

I heard on the news one day that a flywheel had become detached from one of the engines and spun at great speed into a passing underground train with no injuries except shock to some of the passengers. Within ten minutes of me hearing the news I was called on the telephone to go to Rickmansworth with the breakdown train and recover this wayward flywheel. On examination it was found that some of the holding bolts had been loose for some time and all the fleet had to be checked; every nut and bolt on every flywheel. We worked all one weekend to accomplish this.

My next visit to hospital was because of a flywheel. We had to check the oil levels in them on a big exam. This was done by setting the flywheel with the filling plug at the top, removing the plug and turning the flywheel until the oil dripped out. If the hole was further round than it should be it had to be topped up. I removed the plug and oil shot out spraying my face. It was a vegetable oil with some dangerous properties, and even had to be kept off hands. Both my eyes were awash with it. Someone had overfilled the flywheel and it had built up quite a bit of pressure. I was taken to Moorfields Eye Hospital which wasn't very far away and both my eyes were washed out. My right eye was especially painful. I returned to work wearing a patch and was greeted with jokes about pirates and people asking me where my parrot had gone.

On the night shift there were two fitters and two mates. The mates would fuel all the units as they arrived and the fitters would get on with the repairs. The last unit to arrive was about two o'clock. One night I had gone out to see the mates at the fuel point. It was a clear warm night and as we sat talking waiting for the last unit to arrive, we saw a light in the sky. It was in the south, coming slowly towards us. I have no idea how far away it was but we all thought it was helicopter until it shot towards the west. It didn't accelerate, it just went. We were all speculating about what it was when the unit arrived. On the news that day two police officers in Wales had reported seeing a fast bright light at two o'clock. We said nothing, not wanting to be open to ridicule.

The only work carried out on the three roads in the old shed was filling the engines with oil and the radiators with water. The roof was only just clear of the tops of the units as it had been a carriage shed and when all the engines were running the atmosphere was full of diesel fumes which made it difficult to breath. Sometimes a fitter or mate would be on the floor coughing. The union brought in a chap with some kind of meter to check the air and we were all told it was safe to work in there. The staff were very concerned about this as sometimes the visibility was down to a few feet because of the thick diesel fumes.

As the breakdown was used only occasionally we didn't carry much food, only tins of corned beef and Spam and a large jar of pickled onions. We had tea and sugar on board and I would take in a bottle of milk and a loaf of bread.

On the 23rd July '69, I was called back from work early in the morning to get my wife to the maternity wing of the Whittington Hospital which was on Bishops Avenue. This mansion was on loan to the N.H.S. from Gracie Fields who owned it. On my way to work the next night I visited my wife and son, Andrew. Luckily it was on my way to work.

The third time my wife was expecting, we found out a few days before the birth that it was to be a multiple birth. On the 8th February '71, I took her to the North Middlesex Hospital, and went to work. The nurses told me to ring early the next morning. At 0600 hours I was on the phone and to my delight was told I had a baby girl Kathryn and boy Richard, and all three were doing well. I wasn't allowed to visit until the evening visiting time, so I went home to tell my mother and father all the news. They had come from the North to look after the two older children whilst my wife was in hospital.

I had bought a tin of cigars and I had a pocket full of money and, when I arrived at work, I went over to the Boston Arms to tell everyone my good news. I placed the tin of cigars on the bar and invited everyone to join in my celebration and the night went with a real swing.

The landlord and landlady, a retired police officer and nurse, were quite new to the Boston and, years later when I went in there, they recognised me and talked about the party we had that night.

After a few months of going out on calls with a foreman I was soon allowed to take out the breakdown myself, I was also expected to be the fitter and the cook. Because Marylebone had only a small gang with hand jacks, I was missing working with a crane.

Fate then played a hand. Marylebone was to cut its staff and I was the last one to stay. Everyone who joined after my starting date was to be made redundant. At the same time I heard that a Polish fitter at Cricklewood was leaving and he was a breakdown fitter. I applied for a transfer and it was granted, so one of the electricians at Marylebone stepped into my place. He thought I was doing him a favour. He was older than I was but I was happy to be on the move again to a shed that maintained locos as well as D.M.Us, and I would be able to work with a crane which was my main interest.

Cricklewood – bogie fell off.

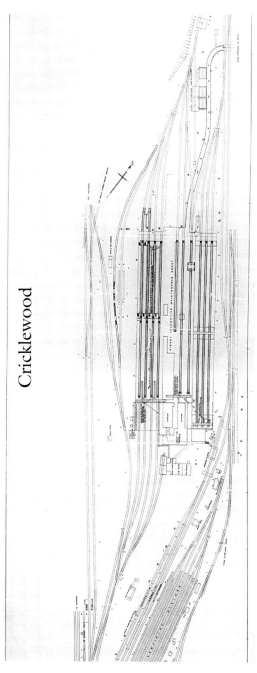

Cricklewood

CHAPTER 6

CRICKLEWOOD 1

Cricklewood was a big shed with everything under the one roof, running North to South on the up side of the St Pancras to Bedford main line. The stores and foreman's office ran down the middle of the shed from South almost half way. These buildings split the shed. At the back of the stores and offices was the area for the locos and in front was the railcar area. The loco roads were one to four and ran the full length of the shed. The South end had normal pits, and the North end had platforms to enable men to work on the engines with ease and move equipment in and out of the cab or through the engine room door.

No. 5 road ran from the North of the shed to the middle by the foreman's office. This was the jacking road with four Matterson jacks which were used to lift a loco off its bogies. They were electrically operated through a movable console and could be lifted or lowered at the same time with one switch. On the North end of five was a fixed fifteen ton crane which straddled the road with no pit at that end. This enabled a lorry to be driven under the crane for loading or off loading anything up to the weight of a loco bogie.

No. 6 road was the drop pit road and this one stopped by the buffer stops of five.

Seven again ran from the North end but was longer and the buffer stops were opposite the stores. On the North end of seven was the wheel lathe. It was the first new one I had seen and was a new innovation, as there was no need to remove the axles and wheels to re-profile them they could be worked on in situ.

Roads 8, 9 and 10 were longer and were for rail cars. They would take a full eight car or two four car units. They ran from the North to buffer stops before the boiler house.

The South end of eight was for the very big exams and the power cars had been uncoupled from the trailers so that work could be carried out on three or four at a time. Once the power cars were on the South of eight road it could be months before they turned a wheel. Because of the work that was carried out on them, almost all the components which were under slung were changed. This was also a good time to repair any body work that needed attention.

The traction at Cricklewood was Class 25s, 40s, 45s, 46s and 47s, also O8 shunting locos. The rail cars were B.U.T and Rolls Royce. The B.U.T railcars were similar to the Marylebone fleet, but lighter with different gear boxes and smaller final drives.

Two hundred yards north was the fuel point, and to the South were the carriage sidings. This was where any unit not needing any repairs or exam was stabled and cleaned.

Between the shed and the main line stood the breakdown train. It was on two roads; the vans on one and the crane next to them. This was because the Midland Region had a rule that 75 ton capacity cranes had to be coupled to the loco. If the crane was required, a loco would pick it up and place it on the North or South end of the vans, depending on where the derailment was. After the derailment was cleared the breakdown train had to be re-marshalled to come back to Cricklewood with the crane once more between the loco and the vans. This always took a while and gave the gang time to pop in the nearest pub.

On the day I arrived at Cricklewood, I met the manager and supervisors and saw some of my friends from the Hampden Club. After a brief hello I was round the back of the shed to check out the breakdown. The crane was similar to the one I saw being built at Carlisle and was a massive beast. Cricklewood had added a runner to the back with an extra water tank and coal bunker, so, from the rear, there was runner, relieving bogie, carriage, relieving bogie and jib carrier. Without the extra runner it was almost two hundred tons.

I made myself known to the crane driver and was welcomed aboard the riding van where we had a mug of tea and a chat. The drivers name was Paddy Lacey and he was getting on in years but, as I was in my mid twenties, anyone over forty was ancient to me. I returned to the shed wondering how long it would be before I was on call.

The next day I arrived on time and was to assist a Scottish fitter I knew from the Hampden Club on an exam on a Rolls Royce rail car. This was new and interesting work as the power car didn't have a gear box but a torque converter fixed to each engine.

As I was a new hand I was on days for a few weeks getting to know the locos and units, and chatting to the members of the breakdown gang. I met the Polish fitter who I hoped to replace on the gang and he said he was going in a couple of months.

The amenity block was at the South of the shed with the locker rooms and wash rooms on ground level along with the shed master's office and the pay office. The shed master was Jim Groom. Upstairs were two mess rooms, one for the fitting staff and one for the drivers. We were always segregated for all kinds of reasons. The mess rooms were fully equipped with cookers and hot water urns. Not many people used them at lunch time as it was normal to cross the main line then through the Brent sidings and go to the B.R.S.A. club for a liquid lunch. It was a big club house just off the main road with a bowling green at the back. The steward must have been an avid bowler and a good gardener because the grass was like velvet. Strangely enough I never saw it in use.

Charlie Grearson was the breakdown foreman and one day he was short of staff and, knowing I was eager for breakdown work, asked me if I would go out with them to Luton. A string of empty coal wagons had jumped the rails. I handed in my work sheets and put my tools away. Two of the fitters who were on the gang were putting their tools away at the same time and said they were glad I was going with them.

We went to the train and it was raining very heavily. The crane was being shunted onto the North end of the vans. The roads on which the breakdown was berthed were quite old track and, as the crane was pulled along, the track and sleepers were complaining of the weight. Loud cracking could be heard from the sleepers and squealing from the wheel flanges as the crane was pulled round a slight curve. I was getting wet but I didn't mind because, as I watched the crane being set back onto the vans, I thought how lucky I was to be back working with such a monster of a crane. People were arriving from home in cars and one old chap arrived on a motor bike. He was George Hernight, the cook, and he worked regular nights. It was a rule that the first person on the train would put the kettle on so that those travelling from home could have a cup of tea as soon as they arrived because they didn't have time to have one at home. I was introduced to the night staff by one of the day fitters and it was barely a half hour from the time of the call. This was a rapid response gang.

The foreman Charlie climbed on board and did a head count, everyone who was supposed to be there was. The guard got us away.

The breakdown train head code was always 1Z99 going to a derailment and 1Y99 on the return. As 1Z99 we had priority and soon arrived at Luton. It was still raining hard and George Hernight loaned me his mackintosh as he was going to stay on the train and make a dinner for us all. The foreman told us to use hand jacks as only five wagons were off and close to the track with none of them badly tangled. A couple of couplings had to be cut with the gas axe and we started re-railing. It was a real pleasure to be working with a big gang again and they all knew what they were doing.

I was surprised at the number of fitters, about five, and only four mates. The gangs at Carnforth and Carlisle had only the one fitter and the rest were mates. The fitter would do any burning and spanner work and examine vehicles to go into traffic or be hauled to a carriage and wagon shop or coach depot.

The gang told me it used to be like that but because of the shortage of mates who would volunteer, more fitters were taken out. We had re-railed three of the wagons when George, the cook, shouted down to us to "come and get it." We all tramped back to the riding van and hung up our wet coats, and took turns to wash our hands in the three sinks. As soon as someone sat down a soup dish and spoon was slid towards him. The dish contained 'Van man's stew'. It was made in a big Dixie with tins of soup, tins of vegetables and tins of meat, corned beef, Spam and tinned beef all cut up into manageable squares. It all went into the one pot and was heated up on the coal fired range. Mugs of tea appeared. We all sat round one long table with a flap down one side. The first to sit down went round the back without a flap. Those arriving later had to sit down and wait till everyone was in place then lift the flap and eat.

It was starting to go dark and after we had all eaten I went with one of the young fitters to get the paraffin lights out of one of the vans and light them. Most wanted new mantles and I quickly fitted them and lit them. We carried the lights on to site and the other young fitter told the gang I knew all about fitting mantles and, because I had jacked coal wagons on many times, I was quickly accepted. As soon as the last pair of wheels had been re-railed we cleared up the site and loaded the jacks, packing and lights into the vans. Most of the gang went to the pub. We may as well get wet inside as well as outside.

The gang consisted of mainly young fitters and old mates and all capable of doing most of the work on the breakdown. We chatted over a couple of pints in the pub about breakdown work and, as usual, all the gruesome or more hazardous jobs got mentioned. I related stories to the gang about working in the North of England and I realised I would fit in and enjoy the Cricklewood gang. On our return to the shed, Charlie Grearson, the foreman, told me to meet him the next day and he would fit me out with a heavy coat and raincoat.

The following morning I went with him to the clothing stores and picked out the said articles. They had been for drivers who had moved on or had the wrong size sent. The fitting staff never had clothes issued like the footplate staff. We had to scrounge everything as if we were the poor relations.

I was put on call and went out with the gang on all the jobs. The most usual places we went to were Luton and Bedford yards, the Brent and Church sidings and round Cricklewood. The Church sidings were just North of St. Pancras Station. On average the breakdown would be out about four or five times a week.

It seemed the crane driver was very wary of the 75 ton crane and never wanted to use it. Usually the Polish fitter, Michael, would drive the crane but it wasn't often used .

Mick, the Pole, had his leaving date and I applied to go on regular nights in his place. This was granted and I ended up with George Hernight, the breakdown cook, as my regular mate. He told me stories from the Second World War. He was in the Forgotten Army up against the Japanese and he had learned to rough it. He was a very willing mate and tried to do all the work himself although he was getting close to sixty.

Because of the likelihood of us being called to a derailment, we would be given small exams on railcars or put on stopped work on the locos. The small exams could be finished quickly and the stopped work would still be there the next day with no urgency.

One morning the breakdown was called to Silkstream Junction. A Class 40 had run through a set of catch points or traps, as some people call them. Catch points protected a junction. If the signal was at red the points would be set to derail to one side anything going passed the signal. It was like going onto a different track but only twenty feet long, then the rails would stop and the loco would end up in the dirt, usually on its side with the rest of the train piled up behind it and sometimes on top of the back cab. This was a way to avoid head on collisions or to stop one train going through the middle of another. At other places, catch points were used on steep inclines. If a coupling broke and the vehicles at the rear of the train ran back down the slope they would derail before they gathered speed and went hurtling the wrong way towards an unsuspecting train. This type of catch point was spring loaded and trailing. The wheels of the vehicles travelling in the right direction would shut the points and continue safely and, as soon as they had cleared the points, they would open.

Quite often a train had come to a stand climbing an incline and, when the driver had rung the signalman informing him of this, the driver would be told to set back and have a good run at it and unfortunately he would end up on the floor. Even signalmen would sometimes forget about the catch points and tell the driver to set back.

On this particular day the train was only partly fitted with brakes and had a brake tender coupled between the loco and wagons. This was a 50 ton vehicle with all axles braked which would assist in stopping the train but, because of the wet rails, the braked wheels slid and the rest of the train pushed the loco passed the signal.

Both the driver and the second man had the good sense to jump out of the second man's side because the loco rolled over to the driver's side. Other times the footplate crew weren't so lucky.

On arrival, we set up the crane by the last derailed wagons. A loco was called up from the shed and the wagons still on the track were hauled away.

There were about a dozen wagons, the brake tender and the loco to recover. The wagons and break tender were no trouble but the Class 40 weighed in at about a hundred and thirty tons, and the leading cab was about forty five feet away from the track. Assistance was requested to re-rail the loco and we were told Stratford would come the next day if we were ready.

We had set up the crane on the up road next to the incident and put the spreader beam on the rams horn then attached two wire lifting hawsers to either end of the spreader beam, and started re-railing. Once the wheels were on the track and we still had the weight on the crane we made sure the axle boxes and springs were in the right position and the vehicle would run.

We had to reposition the crane along the wagons and set up about five times before we were alongside the brake tender. The wire hawsers were removed and replaced with heavy chains. George was keeping us all supplied with mugs of tea and Bovril and we had a stew midway through the day. It was now early evening and all we had to do was re-rail the brake tender and wait for Stratford to turn up to do the tandem lift of the loco. Though the brake tender was only fifty tons going by the label on the side, it was a very heavy fifty tons. Every time we took a lift the crane would start to tip towards the load and we had to pull down the screws on the outriggers and double pack them before we could safely lift the brake tender. The wheel watcher at the back of the crane was getting very worried.

This may be a good time to describe a 75 ton steam crane. The carriage had four axles and a relieving bogie with two extra axles at either end. This was because of the weight. The railway had a twenty five ton limit on all axles. The relieving bogies would fit into the front and back of the carriage via a large wish bone coupling which was held fast in the carriage by two big pins which were operated by a screw. The handle to screw the pins into position was by the right corner at either end of the carriage and had to be turned ninety eight revolutions to ensure the pins were home and locked. Then a hydraulic jack had to be pumped which was an integral part of the relieving bogie to take some of the weight of the carriage, then lock all this with a sliding pin. When both relieving bogies were fitted eight axles were then taking the weight. This was in train running conditions.

It was arduous work to remove these bogies but even harder to refit them after using the crane. When lifting anything heavy without the relieving bogies in position the crane would settle on its carriage springs and drop slightly. This made the refitting of the bogies very difficult. If everything wasn't in perfect line or the same height the big screws wouldn't enter the close fitting bearings on the wishbone coupling. Sometimes we would drive the crane onto a fishplate placed on top of the rail to lift the carriage.

On paper we were supposed to remove the relieving bogies before we took any lift with the crane but it was such hard work coupling and uncoupling. More often than not we would just let the weight off them. If we were lifting over end then we had to remove them.

Just inside the first and fourth axles were the outriggers, two on either side. They were held in position by two inch pins. To slide them out, a two foot long ratchet was used and, although the outriggers were mounted on rollers, it was hard work pulling them out. They would come out about four feet. They were like an H section on its side about twelve inches across and eighteen inches deep. At the end was a screw six inches across with the same size square on the top as the ratchet and that was what was used to screw it down.

To pack an outrigger as big a base as possible was needed under the screw. If the screw was positioned over a rail this was a benefit, we knew the track wouldn't sink. By lacing the packing one way then the other with the longest at the bottom, we would build up a pyramid and on the top place a steel plate with a cup to take the base of the screw. The screw would be pulled down with as much force as possible, sometimes using a long tube which went over the ratchet to gain more leverage. When all four outriggers had been set up we were ready to take a lift. The foreman would tell the crane driver to inch up once the lifting gear was attached and to take the weight. Lifting thirty or forty tons was usually no problem but if the load was heavier or if the outriggers weren't bedded down over track, the packing would creak and sink on the side we were lifting. All the outriggers had to be set up at their full extent, even the ones at the back. The back ones were for any reaction. If the load dropped and the jib was at minimum radius there was a possibility of the crane going over backwards. On heavy lifts we would double pack. This involved placing a long thick piece of packing under the outrigger close to the carriage running along the sleeper ends. We would build up a column of packing on this, finishing off with two thin wooden wedges the same width as the packing. They were placed one from either side so they overlapped. These would be hammered home under the outrigger with long fourteen pound hammers. We only did this on the lifting side. On each corner of the carriage was a bottle jack. They had their own steel plate with a cup fitted to place on top of the packing then, using a six foot bar we would screw it down. On either end of the carriage were two rail dogs. These clamped over the rail with a steel collar which would lock them into position. They were adjusted with a bottle screw and didn't have to be too tight as there was always some movement in the crane when lifting.

If all these were used to bed down a crane there shouldn't be any trouble with the stability. But another thing we had to make sure of was the ground we were packing on. Most of the railway yards had been made on top of fly ash from the steam locos and would give quite a lot. Drains and covered culverts had to be avoided. Most of the cranes which have gone over when they had been packed properly had the lifting side outriggers packed over a drain.

A crane which has overturned is a terrible sight for any breakdown man. If the dogs had been down, the track would be held against the wheels and twisted into an unusual shape. All the gang would have gone back to their shed and only the foreman would be sitting there with a long face wondering what he would say at the inquiry which would surely take place.

The working part of the crane sat central on the carriage on twenty four large rollers. This enabled the crane to slew left or right, three hundred and sixty degrees. At the back of the cab was the boiler. This sat on metal slabs as balance weights. On either side of the boiler were water tanks. On the back lip at the top of the boiler was the chimney. It was hinged and only put up when the crane was working. The cab itself was very narrow. It had no doors only a thick framing to climb over. Over the top of the cab from the chimney to the middle of the gears was a metal canopy. This was hinged at the back and would rise with the jib. The crane driver would have his back to the boiler and look forward over the gears. He was unable to see anything happening on the floor so a good communication system had to be set up. There was a whistle code from one to eight. One whistle was stop. If there were six whistles, the driver would always hang out of the opening at the side and ask how many times you had whistled, so shouting was the best way to communicate and the whistle was just used as a stop signal.

If a man could be spared, sometimes a trained crane driver or the one looking after the boiler would hang out of the cab and the foreman would use hand signals.

When the driver looked forward he would see the derrick rope drum. It went the full width of the crane. Towards the front of that were the slewing gears and in front of that, the main hoist drum and the auxiliary hoist drum at the very front.

The jib was not attached but rested on slides because it was so long. If it was fixed, the crane would never get round a curve. It was a solid jib compared to the lattice jibs most of the 40 and 50 ton cranes had. The sides were solid and at the foot of the jib there was a twelve inch U shaped cut on both sides, called the slides. It was important to watch the slides at the foot and make sure they slid into the right position. When on a bend, the carriage had to be squared up to the jib so it slid into the correct position. The weight of the jib was about thirty tons.

In the early days of 75 ton cranes, before the plates with the working radii were issued, many of the breakdown foremen found themselves in trouble because, with their old small lattice jib cranes, they were used to lifting light loads without the outriggers bedded down. With the new cranes, the weight of the jib slewed at ninety degrees to the track and with the jib reaching out, it could turn over without anything on the hook.

At almost the top of the jib was the main hoist. This had a rams horn hook of solid steel and, with the rope block, stood over six feet tall. I suppose the best way to describe the rams horn is two hooks back to back but made of immensely thick steel. It would fit into the spreader beam which was stowed alongside the jib on the jib carrier. The auxiliary hoist was at the very top of the jib and that was just a large hook. It had a safe working load of twelve tons. Though it was fast to move up and down, it was only used for picking up wheel sets or wreckage to be loaded up. Two rollers stuck out on either side of the jib near the top and, as the jib was lowered on to the carrier, they came into contact with a pair of slides. These were angled forwards so the jib would ease forward away from the main body of the crane. The rams horn would slide into an angled compartment in the jib carrier and the auxiliary block had its own compartment right at the front of the carrier. At either side of the jib carrier at knee height were packing bins. These were for the extra long packing which went under the outriggers. The whole crane was painted red as all the breakdown vans were.

All the working of the crane was on one main drive shaft which ran across the crane. The pistons were mounted on the side of the crane in front of the cab.

The different gears were selected by the driver on a console in the cab. The sliding dogs which mesh the drive shaft with the gears were assisted by twelve hundred pounds of nitrogen pressure, and would go over with a bang. The teeth of the dogs were square with a small chamfer on the corner. They were a good fit and about two inches deep. If the nitrogen pressure had dropped, the dog would not go in properly and would skip across the teeth. This sounded like a machine gun going off.

For safety's sake, after every move was completed with a particular gear, the brake had to be put on then the gear taken out and the drive shaft run in reverse. This was the only way to safeguard having two gears in at once.

Getting back to Silkstream Junction and the Class 40 on its side, it was always common practise when another crane came to assist to give them the easier end. And on this occasion the leading cab of the derailed loco was so far on to waste ground that the crane was moved opposite on to the down road, letting Stratford have the good bed we had prepared for lifting the brake tender.

As it was dark and we had nothing to do, we all adjourned to a local pub for the duration of the night. On our return to the breakdown train we had more van man's stew made by George, and mugs of tea, then to sleep. First class cushions appeared out of the many lockers on the train, and people were sleeping on the table or the long seats or on the floor under the table and in the kitchen. I had seen some palliasses in the packing van. These were used to go between the chains and the body side of vehicles which must not be damaged. They were like large sacks full of straw. That's what I used to sleep on that night.

I woke up to a fine morning and the smell of cooking. George must have been up early and found a milkman and purchased all he had in his cold box; bacon, sausages, eggs and bread. He made a handsome breakfast for us all, after which we had a few games of cribbage.

We received a message that Stratford gang would be arriving at about ten o'clock. We set up the crane for a big lift and, going by the mechanical radius indicator on the jib, we could only lift thirty tons safely.

Stratford arrived and started to set up their crane. I thought they looked a well practised gang. As Stratford was almost in radius to lift they rolled the loco over towards us and got it upright. The lifting brackets were fitted and we were ready to take a lift. The foreman asked me to watch the wheels, so I went round the back of the crane under the boiler. When the crane was slewed at ninety degrees the back of the crane stuck out eighteen feet from the centre of the carriage. This was something to remember when setting up a 75 ton crane. I had to make sure that nothing came within that eighteen feet; walls, buildings, telegraph poles and embankments.

As I was the wheel watcher, I would lie between the back outriggers and watch the wheels on the track. When the crane started to lift it would tip slightly towards the load and, if the wheels started to lift, I had to yell to the foreman and let him know the back was lifting. I looked across at the Stratford wheel watcher. He was a big old boy who I would meet in later years, Bill Wallace. He was sat on a pile of packing and had a shovel stuck between wheel and the rail. As the wheel lifted the shovel would drop. These old boys knew all the tricks.

Because both cranes were set up for a big lift, it went without a hitch and the loco was back on the track by midday. The Stratford gang had done what was required and they put their crane away speedily, then asked us where the nearest pub was.

The Cricklewood gang had to remove the traction motor gear cases and clean out any ballast which had found its way into the motors. We soon joined them and, as we walked passed their crane, I saw the number ADB 966111. It was the crane I saw being built at Carlisle.

The Stratford gang were all getting on in years and liked their beer. After a few rounds we left the pub together and went to our respective trains. The loco off our train had taken the re-railed loco back to the Cricklewood depot. The Stratford train was ready to go and we waved them away. I didn't realise then that I would see a lot more of them later.

We put our crane away and were ready to re-marshal the train when our loco came back for us. We arrived back at Cricklewood at about 1700 hours. We had been out thirty three hours but it was a good feeling knowing we had accomplished the clearing of quite a major incident.

On my next shift I was working on the re-railed loco. It was on the jacking road. Someone had started on it and lifted the loco off its bogies with the Matterson jacks. We checked the centre castings before putting it back together. The traction motor gear case covers were replaced and the loco was ready for traffic.

One of the reasons we didn't change all the brake blocks on a multiple unit was highlighted one day. Someone had enthusiastically changed most of them on a four car unit and when the driver took the train out of nine road for the morning service he was unable to stop, and the train crashed into the buffer stops passed the fuelling point. He was lucky he was propelling the unit out with the aid of a shunter because, as the leading power car impacted on the buffer stops, the rails broke and went up into the cab, one of them going right through the drivers seat. Most buffer stops were made out of old rails and could be connected to the end of a track using fishplates. As most of the breakdown staff were on nights and getting ready to clock off, we were on the job right away. As we cut through the rails sticking up into the cab a loco was organised to pull the unit back onto the road. Only one bogie was off and it was all completed within the hour. A directive was posted that day that no more than fifty per cent of brake blocks had to be changed at one time on any unit. It was because the blocks were rough cast iron and took a few applications before they bedded in.

One Friday night the Cricklewood breakdown was asked to assist the Old Oak Common gang with a major incident at one of the Ealing stations. It seems a parcel train with a Class 31 on the front, being driven by a Stratford driver, was rerouted from its normal path around a train which was stood in the station blocking its way. The parcel train was doing about seventy five miles an hour when it hit the crossing which was a twenty miles an hour crossover.

The driver didn't realise this because he had been overcome by diesel fumes that had leaked into the cab from the engine room. At the severe jolt of the loco going to the left, he came round and made an emergency brake application which resulted in all the vans, eighteen G.U.V.s (General Utility Vehicles) being derailed. They were severely damaged and tore up all the track of the four roads.

They found the driver a quarter of a mile down the track wandering about in a bad way. It is believed that if the driver had not made an emergency brake application the train may have stayed on the track with a bit of swaying. Hind sight is a wonderful thing.

Old Oak Common had an old up rated 45 ton Ransom Rapier crane with a lattice jib and could move under its own steam. This made it look nimble compared to our 75 tonner. We had a problem with the travelling gears and had to be repositioned by our loco every time we wanted to move.

Cricklewood had the loco to re-rail first. As it was still upright, it was no bother re-railing one bogie at a time except for the lifting brackets. They were great lumps of steel strong enough to lift the Queen Mary. We found the best way to fit them was to hang them on the end of the double hawsers from the spreader beam and offer them up with the crane.

Old Oak had started re-railing the back of the train. I believe nine wagons were smashed with wheels out of the horn stays and no one had any idea which wheels belonged to which wagons.

After the re-railed loco was dispatched we started on the London end wagons. The first two were upright and easily dealt with then we were into the wreckage.

British Rail Police and some Post Office staff were trying to recover all the parcels which were strewn all over the site.

It was now Saturday and I should have been going to the Lake District on holiday with my family. I rang my wife to say I was going to be busy and I would ring again Sunday.

The Salvation Army set up a stall in the station with tea and sandwiches for all the chaps working there. When they asked how long we would be on site before it was all cleared we said it would be days so some of the ladies went home and started baking cakes for us.

The vans which were total wrecks and those which could not run were lifted off the railway and placed on the side away from the track. This would allow us to move our crane into the middle of the wreckage, but the track was damaged and buckled so badly that it was unsafe to put our crane on it. A Salmon loaded with track panels was brought up behind us and, after the P way gang had uncoupled the damaged track in front of us, we lifted it out and dumped it with the rest of the scrap, then slewed round and picked up a new track panel and placed it in front of us. The P way soon tied it to the existing track with fishplates and we could then run on to it to get to other wagons. This had to be done another four or five times before everything was cleared.

The following day, Sunday, I rang my wife again and told her I wouldn't be home that day and may not get home Monday.

Though we were on site all the time we had to keep stopping work to let the P way and the signal and telegraph do their work. This gave us time to sleep or pop in the nearest pub which was doing a roaring trade.

Once we had the crane set up the only staff required were the crane driver, a couple of lads to look after the slinging, and a wheel watcher.

George Hernight was keeping us fed with van man's stew and tea but when we told him the Salvation Army had made sandwiches, chocolate cakes and apple pies for us, he threatened to go on strike.

Because the crane was in steam the whole time, we started to run out of coal and water so we had to carry coal from the runner to fill up the crane's coal bunker. The runner had been detached and left with the vans at the South of the station. A fire engine was close by so we persuaded the firemen to fill our crane water tanks. This was a move often used.

It was Tuesday night and most of the wreckage had been removed except one pair of wheels which was missing. People were sent out to look in gardens which backed on to the track in case the wheel set had jumped over a fence.

About this time I mentioned to one of the Western region managers that I should have been on holiday that week. He 'phoned for a taxi and got me back to Cricklewood and I was off on holiday.

I had a close shave as I drove along the M6 on the Preston by pass section because I nodded off and it was only the rumble strip that woke me plus the fact I was driving a big Humber which sat square on the road.

One of the other foreman who took out the breakdown was Freddie Beterson. Both he and Charlie were competent and everyone had confidence in them. Charlie came off call because of ill health and Freddie didn't stay on very long after that.

We started going out on jobs with young R.S.Is, (Rolling Stock Inspectors) who were in charge. There were three in all and none of them had been on the breakdown as a fitter or knew the working of the crane or any of the equipment. They would arrive on site, late usually, when the job was almost finished and do the paper work. This suited the gang most of the time but did lead to arguments on site about who would do the burning or whether the crane should be used, or if we should go to the pub before starting the job or after we had finished.

One day we received a call to go to Luton, one of the R.S.Is would go out with us. A diesel had become derailed at points from the single line from Dunstable, the leading bogie was off and the inside pair of wheels on the second bogie. The job was straight forward. The crane was positioned on the track the loco should have been on and set up for an over end lift. As we took the weight the R.S.I. wanted the crane driver to go higher and higher with the load, not to just re-rail the leading bogie but to try and lift up the derailed pair of wheels on the second bogie.

When he told us what he intended, the whole gang told him how stupid and dangerous it was but he took no notice of us and continued to lift the block. The bogie was at such an angle it became detached and crashed to the ground and gave us much more work to do, fitting the body to the bogie then jacking on the remaining pair of wheels.

About this time we had a pleasant surprise. The breakdown staff who had been on the job at Ealing were invited to a Christmas drink up with the Old Oak Common gang as a thank you for all the work done. It was all to be paid for by the Western Region. This was a lovely gesture and something the Midland Region would never do. It was to be held in a pub close to Old Oak, with food thrown in.

On the chosen night we all turned up and had a good night with the Old Oak gang, each trying to out do each other with stories about our experience on derailments. Only one Western manager made a speech and that was short. If it had been organised by the Midland Region there would have been a queue of managers, who hadn't been at the derailment, wanting to spout.

In the New Year we, the Cricklewood gang, decided that the Christmas party laid on by the Western Region was such a success we would reciprocate and organise one for the Old Oak gang the next Christmas. It was decided all the regular gang would pay fifty new pence a week into a kitty to build up a good fund and this time wives and girl friends would be invited. The venue would be organised nearer the day.

We were kept busy that winter usually at night in the rain and snow. One early morning we were called to Dunstable. A tank had jumped off the single line track, gone over a four foot high banking and was sitting in a field. It was too far away for us to crane it so we would use pulley blocks to pull it back to the track. The pulley blocks were very heavy and Cricklewood carried theirs already reeved so we had to struggle to pull the blocks apart. Each block had four pulley wheels so the force exerted when a loco was pulling on the end of the hawser was great.

Two of the gang, Pat and Jimmy started digging out the bank and, by the time we had coupled the tank to the loco which was going to pull it out of the field, they had cut a gap in the bank to allow the tank an easy path to the railway track. Two Irishmen with shovels had moved a couple of tons of banking and Jimmy was patting down any offending piece of soil on the bed. If medals had been given out for shovelling, they would have won hands down. Jimmy wasn't a fat person but he would wear so many coats and jackets all tied round the middle with cord which was used for releasing the brakes, he looked like the Michelin Man.

The tank came out of the field on the first pull and ran alongside the track. It was soon re-railed with hand jacks. We then had to clear away the equipment. The pulley blocks were so heavy, roped together, that I suggested taking them apart and keeping them separate until we wanted to use them again. All the other gangs I had worked with did this and made it easier to manage. This proved acceptable and we soon had everything stowed away.

It wasn't long before we used them again at Church Sidings just north of St. Pancras station. A box van had gone through the buffer stops and had run into a car park.

Because it was my idea to reeve them as we wanted them, it was my job to 'fight' the two hundred foot long hawser. As the box van was reasonably light, I only used two pulley wheels on each block and that was enough to pull the van back to the track.

We were called to Kettering. This was out of our patch and on Toton's area. A 'phone call was made to check with Toton and, as they were out on another derailment, we went. All the breakdown gangs guarded their areas jealously and we wouldn't go on someone else's patch and expected no one to come on ours unless invited.

Before we departed Cricklewood we had time to go to the dairy between the station and the shed and bought up a load of food for the job. We bought catering packs of bacon and sausages and loads of eggs, bread and milk, so we were well set up and George had his big frying pans out. They were well over two foot across and had seen much action.

On arrival at Kettering, the site of the derailed tanks was over half a mile long. The tanks were 45 ton cement tanks and the driver of the train didn't know they were on the floor until one of the air pipes broke and the brakes went on. Most of the tanks were on their side and one had slid down a branch line.

Empty 45 ton tanks are easy to deal with, especially the cement ones, as they are more robust. Because they had turned over, most of the damage was on the sides of the vehicles and the running gear was hardly touched. I think only the one tank was without its wheels and we positioned it and its wheels off the railway for Toton to recover on a later day.

The smell of bacon and eggs frying could be picked up all over the site, and everyone walking passed the riding van would try and get an invite to breakfast.

We were out over twenty four hours again but had eaten well and as we travelled back to Cricklewood we finished off all the food. We didn't possess a fridge then and ended up eating sausage and bacon sandwiches as we played solo whist.

One of the easier jobs we had was being on standby when the royal train was about. We would sit on the breakdown train with the crane in steam for three hours before the royal went passed. Only once did we get called . It was about two hours before the royal was to arrive at St Pancras. A wagon had become derailed just outside St Pancras. We shot off and re-railed it and it was shunted out of the way. Then we berthed the breakdown train in the station well out of the way.

The royal arrived and some of us positioned ourselves behind pillars and hoardings to watch who was getting off. After about an hour a chap alighted with four or five corgis and got into a waiting car and was whisked away. We all saw the funny side and went back to Cricklewood.

Another time when we were called to Luton was night time and it was pouring with rain. A loco was derailed in the up yard. We set off and, as we approached Silkstream Junction, we came to a stop. The fireman ran back from the loco to the riding van and told us another train had just derailed at the catch points.

We all jumped down and went over to the junction. The footplate staff had jumped out of the derailed train and the driver had hurt his leg. The driver and second man were both put on the breakdown train and given mugs of tea whilst we looked round the damage.

The loco was on its side. It was a Class 45 and six or seven vans were piled up behind it with the rest of the train still on the rails.

We handed the footplate staff over to an operations manager who had arrived. They were complaining that the signal had gone back on them. We found out that this was correct. A new signalman saw the breakdown train on its way and as he had been told we had priority, he changed the signal in front of the goods train so that we could clear the junction first, and the goods train had no chance of stopping.

We were instructed to continue to Luton and re-rail the loco there, then return to Silkstream and start on the vans.

We arrived at Luton and propelled into the Up sidings, just sliding passed the derailed loco with the vans. We stopped the crane so that the outriggers at the rear of the crane would be close to and in front of the buffers. The loco had split the points and was off one bogie. We thought that one lift should do it. The idea was that we would lift the jib, pick up the spreader beam and fit the heavy chains, then slew round and, in a tight radius, pick up the loco. As the jib lifted out of the slides at the front of the carrier it started to swing towards Vauxhalls car park which was full of new cars. We were sat on a four inch cant and the slewing brake wasn't holding. The only thing stopping the jib from swinging round to ninety degrees was the main hoist block sat in its well.

Everything was stopped, the jib was straightened and placed into the slides.

The outriggers on the low side, (that was the lifting side), were packed and pulled down with all the force we could muster. One of the thinner fitters then climbed into the gears to tighten the slewing brake. Once this was done we tried it again and the jib went up to its minimum radius without any bother but it was something that would have to be checked as soon as possible back at the shed. The loco was soon re-railed and the crane and equipment stowed away. It was then the guard's turn to start work and re-marshal the train. This gave us time to nip in the local pub under the bridge. As soon as the train was ready to depart the driver would sound the horn and we would all rush out and scramble up the bank and jump on the train. By the time we arrived back to Silkstream the vans which were able to run had been pulled off and had been taken away.

We started re-railing from the rear because the loco would need two cranes to re-rail it. We would have liked Old Oak to come out to assist but their crane was not big enough for the job, so Stratford would come over again. George had found a milkman again and he supplied us with a good breakfast.

We had all the vans back on and had set the crane up at the front of the Class 45, the same as last time. Stratford would arrive in the afternoon, so we got in the pub first and a couple of lads stayed on site and removed the gear cases while the loco was on its side.

We had a good lunch and, as we returned to site, the Stratford train was arriving. They joked about us requiring their assistance once more and soon we were ready to lift. The Cricklewood foreman, an R.S.I., told the driver to rope up and didn't tell him to stop. Therefore, the block with the spreader beam went to the top of the jib and got stuck in the top pulley wheels. The jib had started lifting which loosened the derrick ropes. We all saw this too late and shouted to the crane driver to stop. The R.S.I. tried to blame the driver and totally lost it. With the Stratford gang looking on we must have looked like a load of amateurs and it was very embarrassing. Between the fitters and the crane driver we managed to get the jib flat along the track and the block on the floor so we could work on it. With big bars and hammers we managed to free the block from the head of the jib but found the pulley wheels damaged at the top of the jib and also on the block. We decided to carry on with the job and say nothing until we returned back to Cricklewood. By lifting and lowering the block slowly the ropes stayed on the pulley wheels and the Class 45 was re-railed.

The pubs were open again by then so the cranes were put away and we all went for a well earned drink with the Stratford gang. The R.S.I. went home in embarrassment. After that Stratford named the Cricklewood gang, 'the gang who lift their jib with the block' We departed the pub on good terms with the Stratford gang and went back to our home depots. As soon as we could, we repaired the pulley wheels by heating them up and hammering out the kinks on the lips and had them looking fine. We also tightened up all the different brakes on the crane.

It was about this time we had a set of German power jacks delivered to us and also set up a blue asbestos gang. Because the breakdown gang were the most likely people to come into contact with blue asbestos, it was us who had all the instructions about it and tried out all the equipment. Everyone had a pair of bright blue overalls with a hood which looked like baby grows. We had to wear Wellington boots with the overall legs on the outside. Around our waist, a big belt on which was hung a battery and an air pump at the back. From the air pump was a pipe that split into two, one pipe over each shoulder to a full face mask which the whole head went in to. The hood was then pulled over from the back and we were ready to work, or that was the idea.

We never got really comfortable with all that gear on but we were told to get used to it for our own safety. I can't remember ever using the equipment in earnest at Cricklewood but it was handy to have it just in case we came across any blue asbestos.

The German power jacks, or M.F.D equipment, was another thing altogether and ended up being used by most of the gangs throughout the railway. It enabled us to do almost anything we could do with a crane, but in the middle of a field. It consisted of a pump set . This was a diesel driven hydraulic pump which sat on top of a three foot square hydraulic oil reservoir tank, six inches deep. On each corner of the tank was a carrying handle and it required four very strong men to carry it even when empty. To help start the engine in cold weather, we were given starter fuses. Each one was as big as a cigarette filter and fitted into a long screw which had to be removed from the top of the engine. The fuse fitted into the end of the screw and was then lit. It would fizz and sparkle and give off heat. It was replaced and tightened, then the engine was turned over with the starting handle. The engine rarely started on the first or second attempt and the gang would take turns at firing it up.

A set of pipes ran from the pump to a console with a manifold underneath. From the manifold four outlets were fitted to the front of the console above four return connectors. This was a two pipe system, power up and power down. The console had four operating handles or levers on the top and four jacks could be operated at the same time.

The set of jacks consisted of five 120/60 ton jacks which had two rams. The first was a 120 ton lift, and the second ram a 60 ton lift. Each ram was about ten inches long. The one twenty ram was about eleven inches across and the second ram, nine inches across.

On paper there was the capacity to lift 480 tons. These were the main lifting jacks for heavy wagons and loco's. There were two 60/30 ton jacks that stood about two foot high, and two 60/30 ton jacks only one foot high, also three step jacks. They were 35 ton capacity and over three and a half feet high. These jacks were versatile with the equipment that came with them. They had a single 35 ton ram, with changeable heads. The first had a normal flat face. If this was removed the step part of the jack could be slide over the whole jack. It was an iron frame like a calliper and at the very bottom a toe about three inches long stuck out at ninety degrees. This toe could be placed under a head stock which was close to the ground, then the ram would extend and lift the frame and the toe would lift the wagon. Another use for these jacks was turning over wagons, locos and coaches which had ended up on their sides. With two steel rope ladders and different jacking heads almost anything could be turned over. The steel rope ladder was positioned under the vehicle to be re-righted at either end and fastened to the bogies and the top rung of the ladder would be halfway up the roof, about chest high. Two of the jacks with a large U shaped head were positioned under each top rung with a steel saddle shaped to sit in the U and also hold the rung. Under the jacks were rockers so they could pivot slightly. We would take the weight on each jack and then power them both up together and place packing under the body side using sleepers and long timbers. When both jacks were fully extended the third jack would be put in position under a lower rung of one of the rope ladders inside the existing jack. We would take the weight and this would release the extended one. The ram was retracted on the first jack, then it was moved to the other end of the vehicle and placed inside that extended jack on a lower rung of the rope ladder. The weight was taken off the extended jack so that it could be retracted. Once the jack that had no weight on it was free, it was removed and retracted. The two jacks that were holding the weight could then be powered up to their maximum height and the whole process of changing over the jacks would be repeated until the vehicle was high enough for it to roll over onto its wheels. The one thing that we had to watch was not to get the pipes tangled up and to make sure the vehicle was packed and well supported. The gang had to work closely with each other as a team.

Another jack was the tipping jack. We had just the one and it was to be used on small empty wagons. It was about eighteen inches high and sat on a square steel frame. A large pin went through the frame and the bottom of the jack, this allowed it to pivot. It had two steel keys to hold the jack upright. The idea was that we would set up the jack under the middle of the buffer beam by the derailed wheels as a normal jack. We would then lift the wagon until the wheels were just above the rails then remove the key fitted on the opposite side of the way we wanted the wagon to go. This allowed it to tip towards the rails. With this came a wheel stop. It was a steel frame about thirty inches long and hooked onto the rail with a high side on the outside of the rail to stop the wheels from going too far and missing the rail altogether.

We persevered with this jack but found it dangerous. Many times it would fly out backwards and the wagon would crash back onto the ballast.

All the equipment was heavy, and the heaviest were the long beams. They were about six yards long and made of aluminium. They were a foot wide and stood eight inches high. There were two of these and they were for traversing locos or wagons towards the track. With the beams came traversing trolleys, four in all, and two pushing jacks that would push ten tons and pull six tons.

When we wanted to traverse a loco which was three or four feet from the rail, after securing the other end with wooden scotches, we then had to jack up the derailed end high enough to get the beam and trolleys underneath, then sit the loco on hard wood packing and slide the beam into position. Sometimes we would sit the loco on the two trolleys, one either side and at other times put a big jack on the trolleys then, with the pushing jack, push the trolleys, jack and loco towards the rail. The pushing jack laid along the beam with its foot in a saddle which was positioned in holes spaced along the top of the beam. The head of the jack sat in a cup on the trolley. If we had to traverse more than a foot we had to keep stopping the move, jack the loco up and reposition the beam. The loco would be travelling on a radius and the beam was straight so the trolleys would start running off the side of the beam. This was always something to be very aware of. It would be better with a banana shaped beam, but you can't have everything.

There was also a small beam, half the length of the big ones. This would sit across the rails under the buffer beam and we could traverse wagons or coaches short distances easily with this. Four handles were fitted to the beams on each corner and the long ones had a hole through the side in the middle in which to place a bar or a jack handle so that two extra men could help carry it.

We heard that a sleeper train had become derailed at Watford. Apparently vandals had broken into a freight train and some wooden packing or palettes had ended up on the track. A train travelling on the up line was derailed and ended up fouling the down. The electric loco on the sleeper train struck the right hand side of the derailed loco with its right hand side at speed and bounced off the track and down a sixty foot embankment. A driver who was travelling back from London on the sleeper was on the second man's seat and was killed. The driver of the sleeper train suffered a heart attack and subsequently died.

Luckily the first vehicle behind the loco was a brake van with ordinary screw couplings, and it followed the loco down the bank with its tail end coupled to the sleeping coaches which were all buckeye coupled, teetering on the top of the bank. If the coaches had followed the loco down the fatality list would have been much bigger.

Willesden and Bletchley gangs were attending and, because no overhead wires or stanchions were knocked down, they were using the M.F.D power jacks. To get an isolation and the wires moved to use a crane would have taken hours and the Railway wanted to keep two roads open for traffic.

One of the gangs decided they had had enough and wanted relieving, so Cricklewood was called. We went by road and were to use the jacking equipment left there by the tired gang. We arrived in a minibus and a lorry and set to work. All the coaches had been cut apart and we would use a loco on the adjacent road with a long hawser to pull a coach along to the undamaged track and re-rail it, one bogie at a time. We had a good system going and three of the remaining coaches were back on the track with two left to do. But then we were told by one of the Midland governors to tip the last two down the bank. We didn't argue but it was such a waste, two sleeper coaches with no serious damage just rolled down the bank for scrap.

The two coaches looked unsafe leaning out over the bank and we thought they would be easily tipped, but no, we had to jack and pack under the lifting side then jack off packing to get the top side higher. We were only using small jacks. The other gang hadn't thought to bring one of their step jacks with them. We did eventually get both of them to roll to the bottom, but it took longer than if we had re-railed them.

We finished what was required of us, and set off back to Cricklewood, stopping at the first pub with a car park. As we sat in there talking about the job, someone mentioned the new electric lights and diesel generator they were using on site. Someone else knew where the depot was that stored them. So we thought we would try and obtain a set as all we had on the train were old paraffin lights.

We found the depot and persuaded the chap there that we needed good lighting and came away with a generator, four sets of lights and associated wiring, all loaded on the lorry. It wasn't really stealing because it was all one railway. On the next day the red paint came out and the generator and metal work of the lights received a good coat of red paint, the same as all the other B.D.V equipment.

British Rail decided to recover the loco but scrap the coaches. The breakdown gang were thinking of fitting longer ropes to the cranes so that we could reach down to the loco from the top of the bank. We needn't have worried about it because it was decided to recover the loco by road.

A steel road about four hundred yards long was rolled out from the nearest road. This was done by the army. They also had to build a bridge over a bridge which was too weak to take the weight of the lorry and the loco. The day came, the crane and the low loader were positioned and the lift went ahead as planned, as it should. The low loader with the loco on the back drove along

Advanced Passenger Train, experimental.

the rolled out steel road onto the highway then came the bridge. The middle was quite high and we could see the lorry would bottom out as it went over the top. It did but also the loco rolled back off the low loader onto the road. The road crane was brought to the bridge and set up and arrangements were being made to lift the lorry and then the loco over, but we were called away to another job.

It was about this time that high visibility waistcoats were being issued and hard hats for the breakdown staff. The waistcoats were no problem but the old boys didn't like the hard hats and would rather wear cloth caps or steam drivers' waterproof peaked hats.

We had a new engineer start at Cricklewood, Barry Gardner. He was a likeable chap and easy to talk to. I asked him if I could take out the breakdown train as the R.S.I.s had no experience and not much enthusiasm. He must have tried but came back with a negative answer. If I was to take out the crane on jobs I must be a higher grade than a fitter. From that day I started to deputise for R.S.I.s who were on leave or sick.

It was usually the outside R.S.I. who I would cover. I would be stationed at the fuel point and as a unit arrived I would check if it was due a mileage exam or had any repairs to rectify. If it wanted working on, I would send it into the shed. If it didn't need any attention, it would go back into the carriage sidings to be cleaned and await its next job. I was still getting called out to derailments but only as a fitter.

The Advanced Passenger Train. (A.P.T.) was doing test runs up to Cricklewood and not many people knew it was coming.

I was at the fuel point one day covering for the outside R.S.I. and this silver train appeared with an unusually long pointed nose. When it stopped there was a hiss of air and the front doors opened and steps came out on either side, and white coated figures descended onto the track both sides. I had to get them back into the train as I wanted to move it off the fuel point as D.M.Us were arriving. We set up a route for it round the back of the shed by the breakdown train.

I informed the office that it was there and I was asked to examine it and make sure it was all in gauge. They must have known something because there were cables and flexible pipe work flapping about along the length of the train. Two of us armed with a roll each of electricians tape set about getting everything into gauge.

It was a regular visitor for a few weeks and some of the R.S.I.s managed to get a run on it, but not me. The chaps who did get on it were all very impressed.

It's a pity that on its first public outing its tilt mechanism froze up. On all the rest of the locos and units the air compressors had a little container with methylated spirit in it by the air intake, and the fumes from the meths. would be sucked into the air system. This was to stop pneumatic valves from freezing up.

The breakdown gang were trying to sort out the venue of the drink up we were to arrange with the Old Oak Common gang, but before everything was finalised a second major incident happened at Ealing and both gangs were out together again.

This time an early evening passenger train out of Paddington heading for Reading had derailed and turned over at speed. The loco was Western Talisman number 1007.

The loco and the first two coaches had slid on their sides with the coaches blocking the up line. The next five coaches were concertinaed in a tight zigzag up the bank on the down side and the rest were sitting on the ballast. This happened just before Christmas.

On arrival we were told that there was only the one fatality, a passenger, but quite a few injured and they were still ferrying them to hospital. The footplate staff were fine but the driver had lost a button off his coat.

I took a young fitter with me to check the coaches, Ian. He was very much like me and loved breakdown work. Because of the tight zigzag of the coaches it was impossible to go from one to the other through the companionway doors, so each coach had to be climbed into. I found one coach tight between two others which were missed by the rescue teams and in one compartment, six bodies. A bogie had come through the body side and landed on them, all men. I told Ian to bring the fire chief and I checked out the six men. It was a sight I will never forget.

This was now a problem because they were all pronounced dead at the scene and we had to take great care removing them. I suggested punching two holes in the roof to lower our chains through and lifting the bogie off them but, as we would have to move some other derailed coaches to position the crane, that was not agreed to. The whole coach would be dismantled removing the two bulkheads with the seats attached and recover the bodies backwards. That was the way it was to be done.

We secured the bogie with chains to limit any movement and a scrap firm arrived to do the dismantling of the coach.

To prove how someone was looking down on the railway, a train coming from Reading should have been passing at the moment of the derailment. The driver of the London bound train kept losing power and was over five minutes behind time or he would have ploughed through the wreckage causing even more death and destruction.

When the loco was checked at the shed for loss of power, nothing could be found wrong with it.

The cause of the crash was put down to the loco battery box sliding out from under the loco and coming into contact with a line side junction box which operated the points. When the box shorted out it changed the facing points under the loco as it passed over them at speed. The railway management immediately tried to blame the last maintenance electrician who worked on the loco for not replacing the bolt which held the battery box securely. I climbed on top of the derailed loco and found the bolt had sheared. It had been replaced but for whatever reason had failed on the move.

The Cricklewood gang started on the London end, the rear coaches and re-railed the upright coaches with jacks as they were close to the rails. Old Oak started on the overturned coaches blocking the up road.

The removal of the bodies took about twenty four hours and we had to wait for them to be moved before we could start on the main wreckage. We caught up on our sleeping and eating with a couple of visits to the local. It seemed a bit odd with all the Christmas decorations up in the shops and pubs and us in our working clothes. We had removed our overalls, of course, but heavy boots can't be hidden.

Once we were allowed into the wreckage we soon made short work of it. We had to watch the scrap men as they would start cutting up good coaches.

The evening before Christmas Eve everything was clear except the loco. It was decided to come back between Christmas and the New Year to recover it, and this we did.

On our return to site, a raft of sleepers had been laid the full length of the loco by the wheels. This was to land the loco on.

We had discussed what our chances were of getting a trophy. We thought the name plate would go well above the windows in the riding van. The number plate 1007 was George Hernight's clock number so, without him knowing, I went to see one of the Western managers and put this to him. The number plate was to be held until George retired and we would present it to him along with a clean chromed body side cutter. This is like a tin opener but three foot long and, as George was the cook, we thought it would be amusing. The manager gave us his blessing.

The re-righting and re-railing went well, then Ian and myself started removing the number and name plates. I was on the ground with a hammer and chisel and Ian was in the engine room hanging out of the body side window removing the name plate. We took them back to the Cricklewood train, and hid them on the runner. Even though we had permission to take them, we did not want to be seen.

We jumped in the riding van just as we got the 'right away', only Ian and myself knew about the plates. I never realised the trouble that that number and nameplate would cause.

It was well into the New Year and I was sitting in the mess room with some of the gang when I was called into the office at about 0530 hours. We all thought it was a callout.

The top man at Cricklewood had come in early and wanted to see me. He had a written description of me and Ian which a guard had submitted. The descriptions were so accurate it was obvious that we had taken the plates. If they weren't returned all the gang would be involved with the police and George would lose his pension.

Even though we had permission from the Western region, the Midland region wanted them to go to collector's corner at Euston, so the Midland got them. I believe the name plate went for seven thousand pounds. I suppose it was silly of us for taking the undamaged plates. If we got the ones from the underside of the loco which had slid along the track resulting in big gouges and letters missing no one would have minded.

The Midland and Western management heard of our proposed drink up and got involved. It was to be held at the Stevenson Rooms at Euston station. Extra money was forthcoming from the management but we had to sit through lots of speeches from people we had never seen or heard of. That was the one thing we didn't want . The wives and girl friends thought we worked with a strange bunch, but we explained who the members of the two gangs were and stayed together. It was nice and a little strange seeing all the men dressed up and on their best behaviour. It wasn't too bad a night in the end and we arrived home by taxi around three o'clock in the morning.

We were called to Sundon Cement Works, North of Silk Stream Junction. It was thought that children had released the brakes on a string of empty wagons and they had run away towards the main line. Because the incline to the cement works was so steep, a set of points was protecting the main line and the track veered away and up a run off that came to a stop above some trees. There were no buffer stops, the rails just came to an end. When we arrived it was a spectacular site with ten wagons in and on top of a load of trees. To recover them we would have to stand the crane on the main line so the job was put back until the weekend.

We set off with plenty of food on the Saturday night. Once the crane was set up we lugged the burning equipment into the trees, couplings had to be cut, and everything had to be treated very gently as some of the wagons were unsafe and could move at the slightest touch. We started by lifting the top ones first. We used light wire strops as the wagons were less than ten tons and by breakfast time we all had a good appetite for the breakfast George had prepared. We finished the job and found we were unable to return to the shed as there was a possession between us and Cricklewood. The crane was put away and re-marshalled. We couldn't do anything so we found a pub and made the best of it. The possession wasn't given up until Monday morning.

Although most of the fitters could use a gas axe, it was decided we would have to be certificated. Ian and myself were sent to Crewe for a week to learn burning with oxy-acetylene torches. Ian had just bought himself a new sporty car so we gave the trains a miss and roared up the motorway.

We arrived Monday morning ready for the course and had the first two hours in a classroom learning all the safety rules. We told the instructor we were breakdown men and didn't want to spend the week cutting up bits of metal in a workshop. At the back of Crewe works were rows and rows of old steam engines waiting to be cut up. It was one of these we were let loose on. We cut everything from every position even lying under the loco and cutting above us as that was a common position to be in. We even used the long reach guns. These were about five feet long with nozzles at ninety degrees or straight. The straight ones were probably the most difficult to use as we had to guess the distance from the end of the nozzle to the metal we were cutting. We didn't want to put the nozzle too close to the metal as a blow back would occur and put the flame out and laying on the floor under a loco isn't the best place to light up. I think the thickest metal we cut through were the axles, a good nine or ten inches thick. We had a good week except for Ian picking up three points on his licence for speeding.

Cricklewood had an enthusiastic shop committee and a strike would be called at the drop of a hat. I was on regular nights along with about twenty other fitting staff and the day shift had all gone on strike. A letter had been left with the foreman for the night shift. As I walked passed the office to clock on, it was handed to me. I convened a meeting in the mess room. Actually all the staff were drinking tea. I read it out and it seemed that the fitters working the overhead crane were not getting paid crane driver money when they drove the crane. This sounded a valid grievance until the crane driver on nights pointed out that his rate of pay was less than a fitter. I thought this silly and said so. On reading the letter again the day shift had walked out just after the lunch break and were going to start work the following morning losing only a couple of hours pay. Most of the night shift came to work on public transport and were unable to return home so would have to wait until the tubes, buses and trains started running again. In the letter the committee had put the voting figures, for and against. I had a quick vote with the night staff and when I added the against numbers to the day shift against it was more so we decided to stay and work. Then one of the mates realised the West Indies were playing cricket at the Oval. Instead of writing them a letter, I stayed back and faced them telling them what I thought of them.

Another social event was the marriage of the daughter of one of the gang. Paddy's daughter was a lovely girl. The breakdown had been stood down that day as most of the gang were invited to the wedding. Nobby, one of the breakdown fitters, was the barman and did me some damage. I was drinking white rum and coke and when the white rum ran out he was mixing all sorts of spirits, filling the glass up with coke and giving it to me. I don't remember much about the night or most of the next day. But I have never touched white rum and coke since.

This Ransomes and Rapier 45 ton steam crane (built during the Second World War) is similar to the Old Oak Common crane used at the two Ealing derailments. *(Photograph courtesy of David Idle of North Yorkshire Moors' Railway)*.

CHAPTER 7

CRICKLEWOOD 2

A work study practitioner's job became vacant at Cricklewood and I saw this as a chance to get a grade. All the R.S.I.s were young and not moving anywhere, and I needed the higher grade to take out the breakdown. I applied for the job and was successful.

I attended a six week work study course at Watford. It was held at "The Grove", a mansion in its own park. There was a dozen of us on the course from all over the country and we got on well, especially in the bar after lessons. The food was excellent and lots of it. The Grove was obviously geared for management. We would travel to Watford on Sunday night ready for the Monday morning start. It was very intensive as it used to be a three month course which had been reduced to six weeks. As most of us were straight off the tools, we all suffered with headaches but that was only in the first week. We were all instructed in the use of calculators. This, to us, was very high tech.

The other chaps on the course knew I was only doing it to get the breakdown foreman's job and joked about me introducing a stop watch as part of the equipment. The part of the course that benefited me the most for the breakdown was the section that covered method study and, though we were given flow charts to fill in on the course, I learned the art of dividing a big job into several smaller parts. This was something I always did on arrival at site on my own before starting. The course highlighted the usefulness of method study. I would check each vehicle to see if it was tangled up with the next and make sure the end of a vehicle which was still on the track didn't become buffer locked when the derailed end was re-railed.

We also learned about B.W.D. (basic work data). This was a way of giving a time for a job without watching it being done. Every action and movement had a time in a book and we would piece all the times together and come up with a time for a particular job. For maintenance of rail cars and loco's at a shed it was no good at all. The best way was the time and motion, i.e. timing with a stop watch. Any good union man would cringe at this and think I had gone over to the other side but, if it is done as we were taught, it's the only fair way. The bonus system was the king and I didn't work it for the management or the men. It had to be open to scrutiny by both sides.

When I was timing someone doing a job, say a component change, it wasn't just the start time and finish time I took, but every half minute I had to put down the work being done and the rate the man being timed was working at. Then I would take into consideration the conditions he was working in. Whether he had his arms above his head, if he was crouched down in a pit and sometimes, if he was unable to actually see what he was doing if he had his arms around the back of some large pipe work. I took all this in and, after passing the end of course exam, I went back to Cricklewood.

I was told by management not to try and introduce the stop watch as they didn't want a strike on their hands. I was on days and calculating each man's bonus at the end of his shift.

The bonus system was a two tier group system, a local affair. Anyone over eighty five per cent went into the top league. This was to safeguard the good workers bonus being dragged down.

On a normal morning I would arrive and calculate all the night shifts times and put them up on a big board so that everyone could see them. Then I would be asked to go to the fuel point as Rolling Stock Inspector and see the returning service in. Then, after the lunch break, I would go back to the office and do more paper work. Sometimes I would be called out on derailments as well. It was a very busy time.

Some of the fitters were complaining about the times for changing cylinder heads on Class 47s, and I had to agree with them. I could never do the job in the time given.

I contacted Derby where all the times came from and asked if they were using some equipment which we weren't. They invited me to go and see for myself. We arranged a date and a time and off I went. After a cup of tea I was taken into the workshop to see a cylinder head being removed and, to my amazement, the engines were all standing on the floor with trestles around them for easy access. In the sheds the engines were in the loco's. The fitting staff had to open the doors in the roof and stand on the drip rail and poke their bodies up through the roof to work on the top of an engine. With very little space, it was very difficult to work speedily. It was no wonder the shed fitters couldn't complete the work on time.

I went back to Cricklewood and started ringing round other sheds and found that most were complaining about the head removal times on 47s. Eventually I found a shed with more realistic times, and they sent down a copy of their work sheets. I involved the workshop committee and we implemented the new times.

Another complaint about times was the new work. One job was fitting flexible conduit over wires to the generators on the Rolls Royce rail cars. I talked to the electricians, one of which was on the shop committee. He knew I wasn't out to cheat anyone after changing the times for the cylinder heads and, surprisingly, he offered to be timed fitting the flexible conduit. I put it to the management that the shop committee wanted the job timing and it was all accepted.

I sat down with him to work out the method he would be working to. This may sound silly but by sorting out everything before we started saved time and arguments later, like measuring and cutting the new piece of conduit cleaning off the burrs and taking it to the job. The next day armed with my clip board and stop watch and lots of good hearted banter from the staff, we started. I was in the pit with the electrician and he was flying, as if he was in a race. I told him to slow down and work normally but he continued as if his life depended on it. I thought he would have worked slowly to get more time. The conduit was in place and I stopped the clock. He wanted to know the time for the job but I had to tell him I had lots of calculations to do first. I went back to the office to work it out and it took longer than the job itself. After calculating his work rate and the conditions he was working in, I thought I had come up with a reasonable time. I went back to the shop committee and asked if another electrician could be timed as I wanted an average.

A few days later another electrician was chosen for me to time on the same job. This time he worked at a more normal pace and, after I calculated his time, I found the two times almost the same. I was surprised but shouldn't have been because if I got the work rate right and added the percentage for the conditions it should be the same.

Actually I should have done more timings on the job to come up with a good average but, after the work shop committee and the management had seen the two sets of figures, the time was implemented with no other timings required. I was pleased with myself over that.

One Saturday evening I received a call at home. A unit had caught fire south of Cricklewood, on the up road. It seems some Chelsea supporters travelling back from Luton after being knocked out of the cup decided to take out their frustration on the train, by setting it on fire. Luckily this was in the first carriage behind the driver. The driver saw the reflection of the flames flickering in his windscreen and came to a stop just before a tunnel.

The vandals jumped from the train and ran off. Other trains were passing on both sides and no one was struck by them. When we arrived, the leading power car and second coach were gutted. Had the unit entered the tunnel there would have been a long list of fatalities.

The fireproof floor worked very well, it was designed to prevent fire from spreading from a bogie or engine fire into the compartment. Nothing below the sole bar was damaged, above the sole bar was a heap of charred metal and seats. The roof, body side panels and doors had all gone and, on the running boards, the wooden step below each door, was a small pile of melted aluminium which had been the door locks. The intense heat had caused the aluminium to melt and drip on to the running board before the doors were consumed by the fire. That night the unit was dragged back to Cricklewood, and the burnt out power car would be stripped of its engines and other components before it was scrapped.

On the Sunday, I was asked to drive a forklift truck around the two gutted vehicles with a television camera man on a palette, lifting him up and down while he filmed the damage.

Ian was getting married and his stag night was arranged. Most of the van men would be there. We met in a Cricklewood pub and had a whip round. As most of the gang were there and mobile phones hadn't been invented for the masses, we would take turns ringing into the shed to check if everything was quiet or if we were needed. It was just our luck that we were required on the second call.

A Class 45 was derailed all wheels close to Cricklewood on a single line. We finished our drinks and set off. We visited an off licence and bought a load of booze first. A derailment wasn't going to stop Ian's stag night.

On arrival at the derailed loco we found that the track had spread. This happened when the sleepers were rotten and the chairs which the rail sat in had moved outwards, resulting in the loco dropping to the ballast. The 120/60 ton jacks were used to lift one end of the loco and the track was pulled back into gauge with tie bars. Once the track was in gauge the loco was lowered back on to it. We then went to the other end and did the same. We telephoned the shed for a driver to move the loco off the damaged track and were told he may be some time. We couldn't leave in case the loco dropped off again as it was being driven off the damaged track. This was a common occurrence when the track had been damaged. We all sat in one cab of the loco and continued the stag night. Every time a can or bottle was empty it was thrown in the nose of the loco. The booze had almost run out when the driver turned up and luckily the loco stayed on the track on it's return to the shed.

Later someone found all the empties in the nose end and accused the drivers of drinking on the job but once I had explained that it was us celebrating Ian's pre-wedding party, all accusations towards the drivers were dropped.

One derailment which was the fault of drink was an excursion train.

The Kings Cross B.R.S.A. club had arranged a train down to the South coast in the morning and back to London in the evening. The driver and second man would cover both the driving turns by booking off on arrival and booking on in the evening to bring it back.

As most of the passengers were railwaymen and their families, the driver and second man ended up drinking all day with their friends. This resulted in the train speeding through a caution at Feltham. The loco derailed and started to climb the slope to the platform, but only the left hand wheels were on the slope. The right hand wheels were running in the air and the Class 47 went over on its side as most of the leading coaches did. All this was at high speed.

The driver and second man were killed and many of the passengers badly hurt. One of the mates at Cricklewood, Jim, was on the train with his wife and family. He ended up going through a window head first and, when he returned to work much later, his bald head looked like a map of the world. He did say how many stitches he had at the time, but I forget now, but it was very many and I don't think his wife ever went on a train again.

The Cricklewood breakdown were not called to that job, but a couple of fitters had to go and remove all the brake cylinders from the loco to be tested at Derby.

One thing which upset me was that two of the shops committee would get two hours each booked every day for shed security. This was at the time when car bombs and suspect packages were being found in London.

I had a plan to show them up as time wasters. They were supposed to patrol round the shed in the morning, checking for suspect packages. I decided to make an imitation bomb out of bits and pieces around the shed and place it under the main fuel tanks by the fuel point.

By stripping down a 4.5 vault battery, I ended up with metal tubes about four inches long. These were to be the explosives. I took one of the R.S.I.'s wind up alarm clock and, along with some batteries and wire, I taped it all together with black insulating tape and placed it in a cardboard box. I thought it looked quite realistic. As I finished it we received a call to Bedford. As I didn't want anyone to see it before placing it under the fuel tanks, I hid it in Barry Gardner's office. I was going to show him the next day and explain what I was going to do so that if the two men from the shop's committee did find it, there would be no panic. I thought that there was no chance of them finding it.

We left Cricklewood at about nineteen hundred hours with the breakdown train and I forgot all about my make believe bomb.

On our return to the shed the next morning, about nine o'clock there were police cars everywhere with blue flashing lights and a bomb disposal team.

What had happened was that one of the cleaners had gone into Barry Gardner's office to clean it and been asked to wash the windows. As he started at six it was still quiet and as he was washing the windows he heard a ticking noise. It was the alarm clock. He looked to see where the noise was coming from and saw my imitation bomb. He ran out and raised the alarm.

I hadn't had time to let anyone else know as we had left the shed so quickly the night before. I went over to the office as soon as the breakdown was berthed to explain to the police, that it was only a mock up. They had realised this by then, but were very annoyed, thinking it was a bomb hoax. They sat me down and grilled me for the rest of the morning. They wanted to know how I knew how to make a bomb, and if I had ever seen one.

Barry Gardner was livid at the time but when he heard my story he soon saw the funny side and vouched for me to the police. As soon as they all realised I wasn't up to mischief it all became light-hearted and one of the officers told me it had been a good exercise and that they had treated it in the wrong way. As it looked so real, it should have been blown up with a controlled explosion. It's a good job they didn't, but Barry's office often looked as though a bomb had hit it.

I didn't pull any more stunts like that again but it upset the two chaps on the shop's committee when they found out I had tried to set them up and, all of a sudden, they thought the bonus must be wrong because I was doing so much other work, outside R.S.I. and breakdown work.

A team of investigators from Unity House, the headquarters of the N U R, was brought in to check all the times over the last few months. The work sheets and repair cards were all found. Luckily I had kept them all locked up. There was a barrow load of them. I didn't think that anything would be wrong but was a little concerned over the weeks that went by as all the checking was going on. Then one day, I had a phone call to go to the office which the N.U.R. were using. I went in and sat down. They asked me about the other work I was doing, then came the tea and biscuits. I thought that this was a first, getting something off the union, but found out later that they had scrounged it all from the breakdown stores. It seems they had found no discrepancies at all and, as it was such a complicated system with the two tiers, hoped I would carry on doing a good job.

The crane had gone to Derby for its routine maintenance and on this occasion we didn't receive a replacement. This was worrying because we thought that if we could manage without a crane for five or six months, the railway would be looking to place it somewhere else.

The R.S.I.s wanted to make out that every job was a crane job and we lost a great deal of work with other cranes coming onto our patch.

One evening in Luton an empty double decker car transporter had been backing up to a loading ramp for cars and the shunter or driver had misjudged the distance and the train had impacted on to the ramp.

The train was made up of long vehicles with articulated bogies. Instead of each vehicle having a bogie at each end, one bogie sat between two wagons. Five bogies had become derailed and were zigzagged along the track. A chap who was one of the R.S.I.s who took out the breakdown lived at Luton and had been called to look at it. He deemed it a crane job and went home. The guard who was on the train was back at Cricklewood. He told me how the vehicles were positioned and I thought we could re-rail them with the M.F.D. I shot off to Luton in my little van to check what the guard had told me and sure enough the job could be done with the jacks. I cancelled the crane and made it our job. By using the loco still on the train, I pulled the whole thing away from the loading ramp and stretched the train bringing the bogies closer to the rails. By using power jacks and hand jacks the job was soon completed and we still managed a trip to the pub. The R.S.I. who lived at Luton wasn't happy but no one cared as it was our job and we had done it.

Our crane never did come back to Cricklewood and, on its return to London, it was rerouted to Willesden who used it only twice in the first year they had it.

I had just returned to work after my two weeks annual leave in the summer of 1976. Barry Gardner the engineer called me and told me the job I wanted had become vacant, but the closing date for applications had passed whilst I was away. It was the breakdown foreman's post at Stratford. He saw how downcast I was at the prospect of missing out on applying for the job then told me he had rung the top man in the Liverpool Street division and told him I would be a candidate, and asked if my late application would be acceptable. It was, and I received a date for the job interview.

It was at this time that the railway had earmarked ten million pounds to go towards improving Cricklewood shed and the plans of all the improvements were posted.

All the fitting staff thought me silly at wanting to leave a safe shed, or that's what they thought. All I wanted to do was work a big breakdown outfit.

Suited and booted and with my wife's blessing, I set off on the date nice and early to Liverpool Street station where the interviews were to take place. I don't think my wife realised how our lives would change if I was successful.

On my arrival I was shown into a waiting room with two other applicants, who both looked much older than me. I had never met either of them before as they were Eastern Region men and I was always a Midland man. It was a long wait but I was eventually shown in. They were keeping the best to last.

The interview was taken by the Area Manager and the Shed Master. It went on quite a while as they asked me how I would deal with different situations. One of the questions was how I would deal with tanks. I asked if the tanks were one hundred or fifty ton, loaded or empty and, if loaded, with what? Also if the bogies were still attached because all these things were relevant in how I would deal with them.

I started to relate how I would recover them from the very start which was the arrival on the scene. I talked my way through the imaginary job, setting up the crane and fitting the lifting chains. When I said I would place ten foot long four by four packing between the barrel of the tank and the chains they seemed happy and stopped me there as that was all they had wanted to know.

I was asked if I would wear a bowler hat on special occasions like the royals and I had to refuse as I would be wearing my white hard hat.

They asked me if I had thought of moving house closer to Stratford but, as the roads from North London to the shed were plentiful and I was living close to the North Circular, I saw no reason for this.

I was told that if I was successful I would be looking after the gas cutting and welding equipment, not only on the breakdown train, but the shed and the D.R.S., the Diesel Repair Shop, over a hundred sets in all. It would mean checking each set and finding them for their examination every six months. After enquiring if they were all up to date and a system was in place for checking them, and being assured it was, I agreed to be responsible for all of them. The interview came to an end and I was told that they would be in touch.

Travelling home, I thought of all the things I should have asked or mentioned and hoped my age would not be a problem as all breakdown foremen seemed to be much older than me with many more years of experience.

A few days later, Barry Gardner told me in confidence I had been successful and would hear from the Liverpool Street Division with a starting date for Stratford.

I thought I had better go and look round the shed and find a couple of routes for my journey to work. On the first Sunday, I set off with my A to Z and easily found it. I enquired where the breakdown was stabled and was directed to the new shed. It was a very old shed and there was no breakdown train, as it was out bridging. The new shed still had a water crane with a big leather bag fitted. Every Sunday I would go there by a different route and it was always the same, the gang was out working. I should have realised how busy the Stratford gang was.

The letter came with my starting date and I had two weeks of saying goodbye to everyone. I had made so many good friends over the years at Cricklewood and I promised that I would keep in touch.

I had managed to get the job I had always wanted, being in charge of a 75 ton crane and a busy breakdown gang. I had no fear about the work because I had worked under good foremen, and working under not-so-good foremen had taught me what not to do in different situations. I knew that I could get on with almost anyone and was looking forward to working with the Stratford gang.

CHAPTER 8
STRATFORD

My first day at Stratford came and I presented myself to the Shed Master. He took me round the different offices and we sorted out the paper work. One of the clerks was sent out to find Bert, the crane driver. He took over from the Shed Master and we continued my walk round the shed and he introduced me to the other foreman and staff. Bert had started work at Stratford after he had come out of the Merchant Navy just after the Second World War. He was well known and a bit of a rogue but a likable one. He could get anything done for the breakdown from the Out Door Machinery department or the D.R.S. and, in the following years, I would use him and his contacts to improve the conditions on the Breakdown at Stratford.

Stratford was a rambling depot and I will try to describe it. In its hey days of steam, it was one of the biggest sheds in Europe with more loco's and manpower than any other regional shed, and most of the staff still felt that they were special.

Arriving at Stratford by train, there were steps down into the subway which led to platforms ten and eleven. Walking passed the steps which led up to the platforms was a very dark tunnel with turnings left and right with doors on either side that were bolted or boarded up. I never did find out what was down there behind those doors.

On exiting the tunnel into welcoming daylight, the walking route turned to the right and steps had to be climbed. On the left were the workshops of different departments, most of which were boarded up. On the right was a small yard that held infrastructure wagons. After about two hundred and fifty yards the walking route turned left and went between derelict workshops, the one on the left being the rope shop. Air raid shelters were still in evidence on the right, these were left over from the war. After waste land on the left was the new shed. Its name came from

Stratford
Motive Power Depot

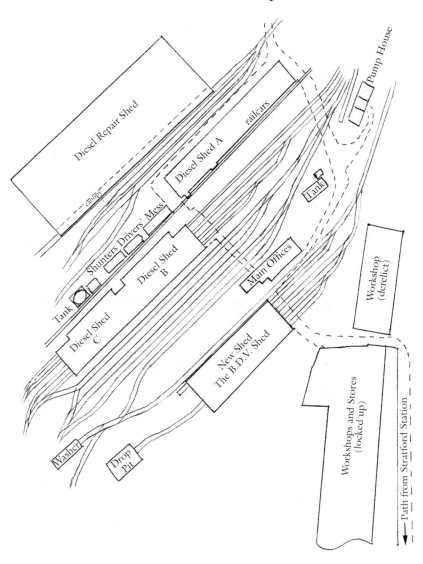

being built after the Jubilee Shed which was Queen Victoria's Jubilee. This was where the breakdown train was stabled. Straight in front were the main offices on two floors. The office block was a very old building. The Shed Master, Chief Clerk and pay office were the first offices along with the bonus clerk and then there was a large office with more clerks and a typist. An arch went through the offices. On the other side of the arch B and C sheds could be seen over to the left and, further away to the right, was A shed. Six roads had to be crossed to get to the B and C sheds. These roads were called steam roads. Its where the Jubilee shed had stood. After crossing in front of B shed, one road went round the back to C shed. In front was the drivers' booking on point and operations offices. To the right was A shed which was the rail car shed for servicing and maintaining the small fleet of B.U.T. rail cars. Looking straight in front across five roads for stabling units, wagons and loco's waiting for repair was the Diesel Repair Shop, D.R.S. It was a massive building remaining from when Stratford had a main works.

In the D.R.S. was the regional stores. It ran down the middle of the shop from the North end to the centre and was a third of the shop wide. On either side were three roads, all with pits. These ran the full length of the shop. The space between the roads at the southern half was taken up with offices and machines, lathes, drills and milling machines. Over the roads at each side were a pair of high capacity cranes for lifting loco's off their bogies. On the outside of the East wall was a canopy that went over a pit. This is where freight liner vehicles had their maintenance done.

B and C sheds were back to back with the stores and supervisors' office in the middle. Upstairs above the stores were the mess room and wash room.

B shed was mainly for the quick turn round, minor repairs and small mileage exams. In C shed the larger exams and component changes were carried out. With four roads in each shed which would take two main line locos on each there was plenty of capacity most of the time. Platforms surrounded the roads and all the pits were raised. This enabled the maintenance staff to work on the bogies standing up and not having to sit on the floor. The platforms made it easier to get in and out of the locos. The whole shed was purpose built for diesels and, with electric charging points and pipes connected to the lubricating oil tank, there was no dragging round forty five gallon oil drums.

The crane driver, Bert, was interested to see his new young foreman and recognised me from the tandem lifts which Cricklewood and Stratford had done together and, of course, he remembered the Cricklewood crane jib being lifted by the block. We had a mug of tea in the riding van and I was introduced to the resident ghost, an old crane driver who had died years ago. I was a bit sceptical at this but, over the years, I realised that there were some things which couldn't be explained, except for a strange presence and an area in the riding van that was always much colder than the rest, even in the height of summer.

Then I checked out the breakdown train with Bert. The riding van was an old Cresley built vehicle. The only one I had seen not in a museum. It was a sixty foot coach with all the normal things for a breakdown gang. On climbing up through the end door there was the toilet and wash basins then through a sliding door, the main saloon with the big table large enough for the whole gang to sit round. After the saloon there was the kitchen with a coal cooking range and everything was covered with a thick dusting of coal. Then, there was my area, a toilet and wash room on the right and a short passage with windows on the left and a row of tall cupboards on the right. These contained all the food we may need and were kept locked. Burt then handed me the key to my office door and I entered. The room was almost as big as the saloon with a large ornate desk against the bulk head and another smaller desk in front of a side window. Beyond that on the back wall was a bed big enough to be a double. The foot of the bed slimmed down and continued round the office as a bench, all well upholstered. With two big windows either side, I would have plenty of daylight and above the bed there were two smaller windows so that I could look at the crane whilst we were on the move. Between the small windows was a cocktail cabinet which I would have to stock, but it did have an array of glasses, probably taken from the pubs that had been frequented. Between the cabinet and the right window was a jigger to apply the train brake. The big ornate desk was only used at major incidents. Drawings and plans would be opened fully and there was plenty of room for many people to stand round it. The office became the command post for meetings and planning on site. Coupled behind the riding van was the crane, ADB966111. The Eastern region didn't have the same rule about cranes being next to the loco. The Stratford crane didn't have a runner as Cricklewood did but leaver hand brakes were fitted to the relieving bogies.

The van behind the crane was a tool and packing van. It was well stocked with hard wood packing and numerous hand jacks which were 25, 35 and 50 ton. On one of the rear bulk heads was strapped an emergency bogie in bits, ready to be assembled when required. It was very strong and had been built in the D.R.S. By the doors at both ends were tall oxygen and acetylene bottles held in metal racks, six of each at both ends. There were rows of paraffin tilly lamps and four mini flood propane gas lights. The lamps were fastened to the handles of the small bottles with a short pipe connected to the valve. They still required mantles and I saw a couple of boxes full of the silk mantles on top of a work bench ready for use. Strong wooden racks ran down both sides of the van and on these were chains, strong hawsers and lifting tackle to be used with the crane. Two cables about ten feet long but immensely thick were pushed under the racks. Bert told me they were for hauling anything very heavy that needed pulling to the railway.

I mentioned to him about all the acetylene bottles and he told me the gang used them for extra light. He showed me some twelve inch copper pipes with connections that fitted the gas bottles on one end and the other end hammered flat into a fan shape but with small holes to let the gas escape. He told me that if we stood a couple of bottles up by the work site we could get a good light off them. It sounded a bit dangerous to me and I told him we wouldn't be using them.

The rear van was the M.F.D. van. Again, there was plenty of packing and burning gear and loads of the power jacks I had never seen before. At the very rear of the van was a swivel chair fitted by the windows which had been put in place by Stratford so that the guard could sit in comfort and watch the track if we had to propel, and he wouldn't need to hang out of the rear door. By the seat was a claxon so that he would warn anyone on the track and there was an air tap and vacuum jigger to use if he wanted to stop the train.

At the other end of the van were over a dozen pairs of lifting brackets for all the different types of diesels and multiple units. Because Stratford was a very active gang, it was often called to other regions to assist and all the different types of traction had their own lifting brackets. It was many years before standard brackets were introduced

As it was getting towards lunch time Bert wanted to take me to the Stratford B.R.S.A. club on Windmill Lane. As we passed The Railway Tavern he said that they open at six o'clock in the morning, as they had a market licence.

I was introduced to a couple of the mates off the breakdown gang who were on nights. I asked what would happen if we had a call and were wanted back at the shed. I was told not to worry as the assistants to the train crew supervisor's, Paul Garry or Terry, who do all the calling out, would ring the B.R.S.A. club first.

No call came and we went back to the shed. Bert would check on his fire in the crane. It was only a small fire just to keep the chill off the water. One of the mates, Ted, who was a relief crane driver working on nights, would pop over and check it during the night.

I went home well satisfied with the equipment and the staff I had met but some house keeping was required on the train. Nothing major but I needed to sort out cleaning and stowing of the equipment.

It was just before bed time when the phone rang at home. My first call at Stratford. I shot off and arrived in twenty minutes, but I was still the last one to arrive.

Bert introduced me to the gang and I tried to remember all the names as we travelled to site. All the mates were about sixty. Only the fitter, John, was around my age.

The job was a couple of empty sand hoppers derailed at Mile End sidings, between Stratford and Liverpool Street on the up side. We arrived in the sidings and I was told to be careful in the dark as there was deep holes in the 'four foot' that the sand was emptied into from the hoppers. The gang went back along the train to get out the hand jacks and lights and I went to look at the job. I saw a row of deep holes and skirted them. They were about twenty foot deep.

The two offending hoppers were standing on their own. I thought I was clear of the holes and didn't expect any more and went straight into one. I was lucky it was full of sand. After I was pulled out, I sat on the rail and emptied my shoes. The hoppers were already re-railed and the equipment was being stowed away. These lads didn't mess about. I took the numbers of the vehicles and saw the reason for the derailment was a build up of sand. I climbed back into the train and was the butt of quite a bit of ribbing, especially as they remembered the incident with the crane at Silk Stream but no harm was done. On another occasion we were in that yard in daylight and I saw how lucky I had been not to fall through an empty hole. Big diggers were running under the tracks and picking up sand and aggregate and loading lorries.

We were called to another job at the opposite side of the main line at Bow Midland. A long string of empty wagons had been propelled along a single track onto some buffer stops not far from a canal.

The track curved to the right and, when the train impacted on the buffer stops, all the middle vehicles, ten in all, were squeezed up and out, derailing them on the outside of the curve and some were on their side. I had the wagons which were still on the track pulled away and the crane, with the jib up ready to work, placed on the track on top of the derailed wagons. My idea was to move the derailed wagons to one side out of our path and work our way to the last one, so that we came back re-railing the ten wagons. It meant us having to lift each wagon twice but it was the only way to complete the job. I thought of re-railing the wagons behind the crane but there was a problem moving the re-railed wagons.

The lads introduced me to a pub just round the corner to Bow. We were still back at Stratford before midnight. On the return to the shed, I had five forms for each job to fill in. I had to record who was on the job, the hours worked, the call out money, what the job was and the cause, what equipment was used and much more. Each form was different and required separate information on it. I thought I may design a new form with all the information which would only need copying.

The next morning we were called to Temple Mills marshalling yard. It was an enormous yard. There was eight fans of six roads each about a mile long as well as the run round roads and goods roads. All the fans were fed from a forty foot high hump and wagons would be whizzing about. My first job was to go to the control tower and make sure nothing was sent down the roads we would be working on. In one of the desk draws in my office were items for signal protection to be used in signal boxes, two iron collars, three inches across and painted red with B.D.V. written on them. They would be placed by me over the long point handles in the signal box. This made it impossible for the Bobby to pull the trigger and operate the points and, in the power boxes that had switches on a desk or console, I had what were called top hats. Small top hats made out of metal and, again, painted red. They would sit on top of the switches and remind the Bobby that the B.D.Vs had taken possession of those particular tracks.

I would then fill in the signalman's log book stating what I had done with the date and time, then sign it.

I had to remember to go up to the box when the job was finished and remove them myself and fill in the log again saying I had handed that bit of railway back to the signalman.

In Temple Mills control tower I introduced myself and was told I would probably be down there every day because of the amount of derailments they had, sometimes two or three a day.

Trains would be pushed from the West Yard up one of two roads over the top of the hump. All the vehicles would have been uncoupled, or should have been. As one wagon started to roll down the other side, the shunter would signal to the driver to stop pushing and let it roll by itself. The number would be read and the road it was to go on determined, also the weight and speed of the wagon. It then ran over one of the top retarders and was slowed down. The slowing down was done by phosphor bronze rubbing strips that were air operated and would apply pressure to the insides of the wheels.

The points at the bottom of the retarder would change and let the wagon run towards the fan it was meant for. Then another retarder would would slow it down more so that it would just trundle down the rest of the slope, through the points to its designated road and come to rest along with the other wagons, to be made up into a train in the main yard.

That was the idea and most of the time that's what happened, but if one of the retarders was slow to operate it would miss the vehicle it should be braking and the vehicle would fly down the track, hitting the other wagons and derailing them or itself. Sometimes if this happened and the wagon was on an empty road it would run through the yard, under Ruckolt Road bridge and into the East Yard.

Occasionally the retarder would operate too fiercely and the pressure would squeeze the wheels of a light wagon off the track. If the points didn't move across fast enough, the first pair of wheels would run over them and then the points would change under the wagon, sending the second pair of wheels down a different road and the wagon usually ended up crossways or on its side. Those are only some of the mechanical faults that could cause a derailment, but when the human element is included, the weather and the track conditions, there was plenty of scope for derailments.

Stratford was surrounded by railway yards. The two freight terminals, Stratford International, and London International. Stratford Market, Thornton Fields Carriage Sidings, Bow, Manor Yard and the Leyton Ballast hole where all the infrastructure trains were made up. We were out day and night at the end of 1976, and I was getting bogged down with the paper work and trying to remember all the different jobs, as we would be called from one to another. At the start of 1977 I decided to keep a log of all the jobs we attended and each page would have all the information I needed to fill in the reports. From January '77 until I left Stratford, I dealt with over three thousand seven hundred and fifty calls and I have every one logged.

About this time I received a visitor. He was a high ranking officer in the Territorial Army, and looked splendid in his uniform. He asked me if I had thought about joining the T.A. and I told him I didn't have enough time to go part time on anything. He told me that because of my job as Breakdown Foreman I would soon have a commission and be involved with the railway section of the T.A. I thanked him for asking but I had no chance of getting time off call.

One day as we had a rare quiet spell, Burt told me that before I arrived at Stratford a film company was looking to make an action film. They were looking at the breakdown and the fire brigade and it was a toss up between the two. Then the British Railway Board decided it would be better if rail crashes were not highlighted on the television. That's when London's Burning started.

CHAPTER 9
1977

From 11th January to the end of December we dealt with two hundred and eighty seven calls, the majority being at Temple Mills Marshalling Yard or within half an hours travel of the Stratford shed.

The gang consisted of one fitter, John, the crane driver, Burt, and seven mates. There was a deputy fitter, Dave, and two deputy mates. With this number of men we were able to always go out with a full gang, even if one or two men were unavailable due to sickness or annual leave.

A spare tool van was always kept available with hand jacks and packing in case a derailment occurred on the shed when we were out. This enabled one of the foremen to deal with a small derailment in the shed or fuel point that would be blocking other locos using a scratch gang off the shift.

Early in January a replacement M.F.D. van arrived. As it was to go on the back of the train, windows were fitted in the back bulkhead by the Diesel Repair Shop, along with packing racks and holding bolts and brackets were fitted to the walls. I had marked where I wanted them fitted to hold the equipment securely.

On 19th January we were on stand by for a royal and, as it was such a rarity to be called, I decided to use the time to carry out some outstanding jobs. I had the new M.F.D. van and the existing one put side by side and the gang transfer all the equipment from the old to the new. As the new van was being shunted on to the train, the guards seat was being bolted down and the job was completed. It was all done whilst we were on stand by and the old van 321088 could then go for tyre turning. It required attention because a hand brake had been left on which resulted in a pair of wheels having flats on.

Temple Mills Hump

Three roads to each King and Queen retarder from the West Yard

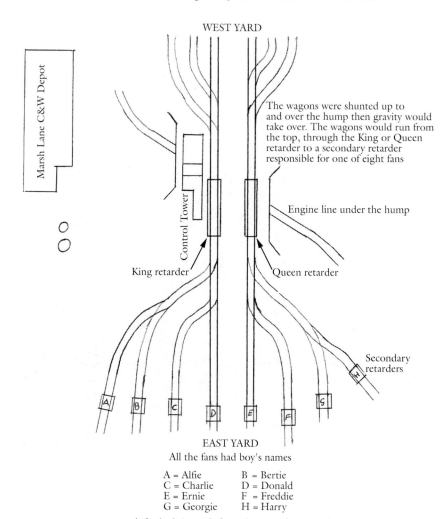

WEST YARD

Marsh Lane C&W Depot

The wagons were shunted up to and over the hump then gravity would take over. The wagons would run from the top, through the King or Queen retarder to a secondary retarder responsible for one of eight fans

Control Tower

Engine line under the hump

King retarder

Queen retarder

Secondary retarders

A   B   C   D   E   F   G   H

EAST YARD

All the fans had boy's names

A = Alfie	B = Bertie
C = Charlie	D = Donald
E = Ernie	F = Freddie
G = Georgie	H = Harry

each fan had six roads from the secondary retarder

At 0300 on 17th February we were called to Temple Mills at the hump end. Seven ferry vans had derailed and lock buffered with one on its side down the bank from the hump. They were blocking the down goods road, the Manor Yard to the down goods, and the two arrival roads to the hump. We departed the shed within the half hour allowed but were held a couple of hundred yards back from the job as the derailed vans had fractured a gas pipe under the track.

As the rain was pouring down we stayed in the riding van and hoped it would fair up. It didn't but we started the recovery at about 0600. At 1400 there was just the van on its side to recover when we received a request to go to the B.R.E.L. sidings as a freight liner wagon DB994784 had derailed blocking all roads.

As we had all the tracks clear in the Mills, the Yard Manager didn't want us back to recover the one van because if we departed to the B.R.E.L. sidings he could use the roads that the breakdown train was standing on, and wouldn't want to give them up on our return. As the ferry van was well clear of the tracks we would leave it there until Saturday 19th.

On the Saturday we departed the shed at 0800 prompt but had to go to the cattle dock first. The cattle dock was at the opposite end to the hump in Temple Mills and it was on our way. A bogie bolster had gone down two roads and was spread over many, from E.3. to the cattle dock. By 1000 the bogie bolster was clear and re-railed and we continued to the West end of the yard.

One good thing was the weather, it was a lovely crisp sunny morning. The crane was set up and, as the van was empty, we used only long light chains. As the wheels were towards the track and the banking it would be awkward to right the van and may be dangerous removing and refitting the chains to take a straight lift to put it back on the track.

I was going to re-rail it in front of the crane so we picked it up as it was and slewed it round across the track and laid it in front of the crane then rolled it towards us and, when it was stood on its wheels, I had a straight lift taken. As soon as the wheels were clear of the ground the van could be turned in line with the track and re-railed, making sure that the springs and axle boxes were all in position.

By midday we started to put the crane away and get the train re-marshalled and had time to go to the Antelope pub which was one of Burt's many locals.

On 22 February 1977 at 1220 we were called to Poplar Dock. A bogie bolster had derailed right next to the water. The crane had to be shunted out of the train because of a steep sloping tunnel we had to travel through. We would have been fine going into the tunnel and out of it but it was the middle bit which was problematical where the slope changed from downwards to upwards. The crane, being so long, would have become stuck against the roof so it was knocked out and left at the shed. Silvertown was another place we couldn't take the crane for the same reason.

On 3rd March we had to prepare the crane for a wash out. This was just Bert and myself with a fitter and mate from the Out Door Machinery Department. O.D.M. Syd the foreman of the O.D.M, had been a breakdown foreman at Stratford for a while and we had a good working relationship. Anything for the crane and the BDVs was always top priority.

Once the boiler had been washed out and the fusible plug changed, the fire bars had to be taken out and examined as it was a good time to work on the crane when it was cold because it was most often in steam or warm ready to be steamed up. The whole job was usually finished in two or three days and the boiler inspector would pressurise it and do his checks and, once he was happy, everything would be put back and the crane would be shunted back into the train.

I had been on a couple of site meetings at Battlebridge which was on a single line from Wickford Junction to Southminster. A few weeks before I arrived at Stratford a train of twenty sand hoppers had derailed. On arrival at the derailment all that could be done was to dump the wagons in a field next to the single line. The farmer was getting annoyed at all the wreckage being in his field and it was arranged for us to go out on Saturday night 12 March '77 and recover as many as possible and be away clear by Sunday night. We would return the next weekend and complete the task. We would have with us a low loader on the back of the train and re-marshal at Wickford. The loco would then propel the train to site. The formation would be riding van leading, then the tool vans. Behind them would be the crane with the jib leading and behind the crane the low loader. The loco 31013 would push us to site from Wickford.

On the morning of Saturday 12th March at 0935 we were called to the freight liner terminus. Three freightliner vehicles B601325, B603139 and B602366 had derailed all wheels. The road next to the derailment was unoccupied and the vehicles had no boxes on them so I ran the crane beside the wagons with the jib up and without outriggers and quickly re-railed them. The job was finished by 1230 and I took some of the gang over to Cricklewood in the ODM lorry, whilst the train was taken back to Stratford. I had been worried that the lighting we had on the train was inadequate so arranged for us to use the electric generator and lights we had obtained when I was at Cricklewood. I intended to return them after I had finished at Battlesbridge. We were back at Stratford by 1600 and loaded the generator and lights on to the low loader and strapped them down.

I went home and returned for the 2300 depart. Most of the gang had spent the evening in the B.R.S.A club. On pre-arranged weekend work it was normal for everyone to provide their own breakfast and cook it themselves. It was amazing what some of them would eat. The plates were very large but Ted would always need two to get all his food on. On this occasion I managed to get some money from the Shed Master to buy some fresh food for the Sunday dinner. John took the money and bought a massive joint of beef and potatoes and vegetables to go with it. His wife

19th February, 1977.

19th February, 1977.

19th February, 1977.

cooked the meat earlier so that it would just need warming up. The bags of food were stored in my office, which was like a fridge, and off we went.

After re-marshalling at Wickford we arrived on site half a mile passed Battlesbridge station at 0200. The loco pushed the train passed the field full of wreckage. The crane was uncoupled from the vans and all the hand brakes on the vans were screwed down.

Burt soon had steam up and the steam brake working. The loco drew away with the low loader and we set up the crane. I had Ray look after the lights and, with all four lights working, we had plenty of illumination and some of the gang would complain about being blinded by so much light.

The idea was that we would load a sand hopper upsidedown on the low loader and the loco would run with it to opposite the large area of waste land by the car park at Battlesbridge station. A road crane would remove the hopper and put it on the waste land to be loaded up and taken away on a later date. Some of the hoppers still had wheel sets in place but most were missing. The first hopper with a pair of wheels in place was going to foul a foot bridge so John climbed up on top and, with the gas axe, cut them free and we put them to one side to be dealt with later.

When the loco took the scrap hopper away, I would slew the crane round with the chains hanging into the field and pick up another to be loaded and have it hanging over the track ready for the return of the low loader. We had a good system working and I let the gang go two at a time to make and eat their breakfast. When it came to my turn, John was cutting the wheels off the next hopper and by the time I was back on the floor the hopper was on its way to Battlesbridge.

The guard would bring down to site the big tea pot and mugs and keep us supplied with hot drinks. The road crane driver was going to leave at midday and his relief wouldn't be on duty until about 1400 so at 1200 we knocked off and after a quick wash went to a pub just down the bank on the up side. We left Albert to prepare the Sunday dinner and, of course, we were back later than expected. The food was good and there was plenty of it. Albert had decided to make some fruit salad with catering tins of peaches, pears and pineapple and told us he had found some custard to put on them. Bert said he thought he knew all the food we had in the big cupboards and had never seen custard. When Albert showed us the big cardboard drum, we found it was mustard powder. He was making custard out of mustard. Most of the label had rubbed off the drum. There was much ribbing after that. Another time Albert was doing the cooking we found him mixing frantically some powdered potato to make some mash but we found it was powdered milk and he couldn't understand why it wasn't thickening up.

The new road crane driver showed up and we continued working through the afternoon. It was so cold that the lads had built a big fire out of the broken sleepers from the derailment. At 2000 we had recovered fifteen of the hoppers and the road crane had placed them in neat rows. We put the crane and lights away and coupled up the train to return to Stratford. The guard said he would propel the train to Woodham Ferrers and re-marshal it there, giving us time to return to the pub and this time Albert went with us.

We arrived back at Stratford at 0030 on Monday morning and were called out at 1000 to a pair of wagons derailed and lock buffered in Temple Mills F fan. Then a loco 31015 had a heavy impact on the buffer stops at the back of C shed, opening a gap in the rails of about twenty feet under the loco. By 1200 we had the loco on a good bit of track and we were on our way home.

On the following Saturday, hoping for a quiet day, we were called to No 47 road in Thornton Fields. Thornton Fields is just south of Stratford and the carriage sidings for Liverpool Street. One GUV, W86578 had derailed just the one pair of wheels and, from the time of the call to arriving back at Stratford, it took one hour and forty minutes to re-rail.

That night we departed the shed just after 2300 and re-marshalled again at Wickford. On arrival at Battlesbridge I was told that the road crane driver wouldn't be on site until 0900 Sunday morning. Everyone had a good sleep and breakfast and by 0900 the first hopper was loaded on the low loader and was on its way to Battlebridge car park. The fifth and last hopper was sent down the line then we started to load up the wheel sets and soon had them all clear. It was midday and we all went out for Sunday lunch.

The guard re-marshalled the train at Woodham Ferres but we were held at Wickford until midnight because of an engineering site possession between us and Shenfield. The breakdown train was stood at the south of the up platform. On the other side of the platform was the Wickford B.R.S.A. club. This was good fortune at its best.

On 23rd March at 0100 we were called to Roydon. One of the wagons on the Croft to Leyton, a Dogfish DB 993000, had a broken axle. The wagon had run along with a hot box and the stub end of the axle had burnt away. We built up the emergency bogie and placed it under the head stock, then strapped up the offending wheels. It was then shunted to a loop by our loco on the B.D.Vs to be recovered later.

On the 26th March at 1745 we were called to Southend Victoria. A nine car electric unit was going into the Klondyke sidings and the first three coaches became derailed. E65221, E65421 and E65621 were blocking the up and down main and the sidings. The message I was given was that the overhead wires were down. I had Bert ride on the crane from Wickford and get steam up so that we could start as soon as we arrived but on arrival not a wire was down or a stanchion touched. The overhead line supervisor told me it would take at least eight hours to slew the wires I wanted moving, and just as long to put them back. Looking at the job I could see that the leading bogie of the leading coach had travelled on the correct track towards the sidings but the trailing bogie had split the points and gone towards the down main. The rest of the train had followed the derailed bogie, resulting in the next two coaches becoming derailed but close to the track.

The Klondyke sidings were about ten feet above the main line on the down side, and the leading coach was reared up from the main line into the sidings. The front of the coach was about thirty feet away and if we didn't use the crane it would have to be traversed that distance and also downwards. The second and third coaches were easy enough to re-rail with hand jacks or M.F.D. It was the first one that gave me concern. I decided to re-rail all three vehicles with the M.F.D. It meant lifting the high end of the leading coach and traversing it towards the main. Jacking something up a bank is much easier than jacking it down. I had the bogie strapped tightly to the body of the coach. This was to cut down the distance we had to lift it to clear the wheels off the ground or packing. All the play in the suspension had to be taken out of the bogie. Using just one 120/60 ton jack sitting on a trolley on top of a long beam, everything was set so that the jack would extend one ram before the second ram took the weight and lift in the centre of the head stock. By having more jack ram to retract than to lift, I hoped to be able to drop the coach in a controlled manner. The beam would have to be reset many times but I could see it could be done. It would be quicker than waiting for the wires to be moved.

The Stratford gang were probably one of the best when it came to using the crane or hand jacks. The way they used the M.F.D., though, was a surprise to me. I had the pumpset and control desk in place along with the beam, trolley and jacks. I then had them couple the pipes whilst we were waiting for the overhead lines to be switched off. I was given the C form at 2210 and saw the earthing cables. We were ready to start. The diesel pump was started eventually, with all the gang having a turn at firing it up. I had pipes from the number one control handle going to the pushing jack that would push the trolley, the big jack and the front of the coach along the beam. The big 120/60 ton jack was coupled to the number four control handle. I had to shout "Up on four!" because of the noise of the diesel pump, and nothing happened. The noise from the engine changed but the jack didn't move. The gang didn't like using the M.F.D. equipment and were complaining about it. I was stood in the pouring rain in the middle of the night with a gang that was close to mutiny, and the jacks didn't work. I started to check on the pipes and found them to be incorrectly coupled. It was now my turn to start complaining. There was a colour code to assist in the coupling. Each pair of pipes were tied together, and each pipe would have red on both ends or blue. I found someone had coupled red to blue and, when I asked who it was, I found it was Albert. He thought red should fit with blue. It was then I realised that the gang hadn't had any real training on the use of M.F.D. With all the pipes coupled correctly the job went well and we traversed the front of the driving coach down in steps towards the main line. I had to make sure the beam stayed horizontal at all times or the trolley would have run away down the beam with disastrous results.

It was 0500 when I handed back the C form to the overhead line supervisor, allowing him to liven up the wires. This is done when the job is completed and all the equipment stowed away.

Because the juice had been turned off from the night before, electric units were all over the system and not in the right place. The B.D.V.s were shunted into the back of the station and we were told we wouldn't get a path back to Stratford until midday. I sent Kevin off to find a milkman and purchase enough food for breakfast. Whilst we were waiting I sat in the saloon with the gang and asked them about any training that they had had on the power jacks. They told me they had made a training film but just did what they were told.

It was 1230 when we departed Southend and I had much to think about to get the gang trained up to the same standard with the M.F.D. as they were with the crane. On our return to Stratford I was told a replacement crane was stabled in Temple Mills. Our seventy five ton crane was to go to Derby for its main works exam, and to be dieselised. I had Bert take the trip loco to the Mills and bring it to the shed and berth it outside the New Shed.

At 0015 on 29th March a call came to go to Channelsea. A train of car flats had became lock buffered round the tight curve. As the long wheel base wagons were negotiating the S bends, the driver had stopped at the signal box to hand over the train to his relief. The act of stopping the train on the straight air brake meant the loco would stop but the wagons momentum kept pushing and even 18 inch wide buffers would slip passed each other on a tight bend. Luckily the Bobby was watching the train and saw the car flats lurch sideways as the buffers slid passed each other. He had the relief driver go and check the train. It didn't take us very long to unlock the buffers, and I went up to the box after the train had continued on its way and was told by the Bobby that long wheel base wagons often became lock buffered when they stopped at the signal box. If the train had set off with lock buffered wagons it would have certainly derailed further along the track.

I stayed at work after we returned from Channelsea and had a good sleep and at 0800 we started to change over the equipment carried on the seventy five ton crane to the forty five ton crane. We transferred the wooden packing which was for under the outriggers and the different chains which we used.

I sent a letter to the Operation's Manager asking if he could arrange to change over relief drivers at the country end of platform ten instead of at the signal box which was at the London end of the platform. By doing this the wagons would be off the tight curve and on the straight line. I had a meeting with him and explained what was happening to the vehicles and he agreed.

Bert had been warming up the forty five ton crane the day before and when we came to try it out there was steam leaking from everywhere. The crane was in a dreadful state. I had no paper work for it and didn't know when it last had a boiler inspection or a washout. I think the other gangs who had had it when their own crane was at the works didn't do any maintenance on it or even use it.

It took us and the Out Door Machinery Department a few days to get it into some kind of shape before I put it in the train.

I was trying to get a forty five ton tank so that the gang could practice at turning a vehicle over with the M.F.D. step jacks. I was promised one soon but I didn't make any arrangements for a weekend of training because I knew it would take some time to arrive.

In April we used the forty five ton crane four times in Temple Mills. The crane was built by Cowans Sheldon, the same as our big one, but had a lattice work jib and was very temperamental. Both Bert and Ted had driven similar cranes and on 1st May we were asked to recover the Dogfish that was on the emergency bogie in the Royden loop. The call was at 0400 and we would meet carriage and wagon fitters on site at 0600. We were on time but there was no sign of the promised C&W staff.

The Dogfish on the emergency bogie was slowly shunted at walking speed from the loop to the C.E.G.B. (Central Electricity Generating Board) sidings, out of the way of the main line and overhead wires. We used the crane to lift the wagon off the emergency bogie which was stripped down, greased and stowed away. We then removed the damaged wheelset and put a new set in place which had arrived by road. We were back at Stratford by midday. I told the C&W the job was completed but it would need examining before the red cards were removed.

On 3rd May we were called to No. 1 road in E fan, Temple Mills. A string of six loaded Esso petrol tanks had became derailed and were tangled up with each other. I thoroughly checked for any leakage before John started cutting away the couplings and stepladders that ran up the ends and, with the crane chugging away, we soon had all six re-railed, just by lifting one end at a time.

The crane was slow at making steam so I arranged to have it washed out on 20th May. As we were knocking the crane out at 0810 we received a call to the Manor Yard where the shunting loco 08519 had derailed all wheels. Within twenty minutes it was re-railed using hand jacks and we were back at Stratford by 1000. The crane washout was completed and the next day, on the second call at 0855, we used the crane to transship a load of channel iron from one damaged vehicle to a good one. The crane was making steam quickly after having its tubes washed out.

On 14th June the first call was at 0500 to Temple Mills. A loco 31006 was derailed all wheels number one bogie. The job done, we arrived back at Stratford and at 0755 we had the second call to the Mills. A hopper E307144 had derailed all wheels in the Manor Sidings. At 1140 the breakdown vans were called to Chingford an E.M.U. E75477 had derailed all wheels on the leading bogie. At 1455, we departed Chingford and made our way to Romford where another class 31, 31002 had derailed all wheels one bogie. We arrived back at Stratford just before 2000. The reason for the two locos and the unit derailing was driver error and the hopper had run too fast through the retarder and had impacted on a string of hoppers.

On 13th July, I was at home when the call came at 2055. Paul, the assistant who does the calling out, told me that I had a right pile up to deal with at Broxbourne Junction. Eight Dogfish and Catfish had derailed and spread across the up and down main lines, knocking down signals and overhead gantries which supported the wires, bringing the wires down. We didn't arrive until just after midnight because the electric multiple units which were between Stratford and Broxbourne had to be cleared out of the way first. I don't know what happened to all the passengers but I imagine they finished their journey by buses which would have been hired by the railway.

Two of the Dogfish were upside down and one had gone down the bank. Because the wires were down we could start immediately we arrived. I was getting the paper work for the isolation sorted. I still had to have a permit to work under the wires even though the wires were down. The Class 31 which had hauled us to site 31133 put the riding van to one side and the forty five ton crane then had easy access. I had my C form from the overhead supervisor and we made a start. Four of the wagons were runnable and we re-railed them. The other four were so badly damaged that we had to dump them down the bank to be recovered later. One of the Dogfish that we dumped, DB 983548, had lost a tyre and that was the cause of the derailment. By 0820 all the wreckage had been cleared and we started to put our train back together and, after handing back my C form, we departed site at 1015, leaving space for the overhead line train to come in and the signal and telegraph department to put up a new signal.

Another busy day was the 19th, six days later. We had five calls that day. The first was at Stratford at 0730, and the last was at Stratford finishing at 2140. In between we went to the hump at Temple Mills, Bow Midland and Broxbourne again.

On 21st July we were asked to remove a bogie and gearbox from a tracklayer, DB965247. The operator of the tracklayer had everything uncoupled and all we had to do was lift the tracklayer off the bogie. The bogie was put on the back of the lorry that had brought the new one. Before we could refit the new bogie we were called to Stratford Market. A guards brake B954339 had split the points and both sets of wheels were on the ballast. The guards brake was speedily dealt with and the gang introduced me to a new pub only twenty feet away from the derailment. As all the gang liked their drink, I would use the licensing laws to my benefit. The pubs would shut in the afternoon at 1430 so, if it was getting close to closing time, I would tell them we could have a drink after the job was finished. This was a good incentive to the lads to get the job finished very quickly and we always managed a few pints. We returned to the shed and completed fitting the new bogie to the tracklayer.

On 26th we returned to Broxbourne after re-railing a couple of wagons in C fan at Temple Mills. We weren't to recover them but sheet them up with a load of wagon sheets. The railway didn't like the passengers seeing the Catfish and Dogfish dumped by the side of the track.

August was a reasonably quiet month with only sixteen derailments, but on the 29th we were called out of our patch to East Ham Car Sheds. East Ham was on the Ripple Lane patch but didn't have a supervisor to take them out. It was only one coach of a four car E.M.U. and took under an hour to re-rail.

The fourth job in September was on the fifth day of the month, and at 1925 the call came that we should go to Temple Mills hump. A box van had jumped off the secondary retarder and was crossways blocking F fan. When we arrived we were stopped a couple of hundred yards away from the job. The Yard Manager climbed on board the riding van to see me. The box van B784644 that was derailed contained explosives. We had to wait for someone from the R.A.F. to check it out before we could start to re-rail it. The chap would be arriving by helicopter and it would be some time before he got there.

We decided to go to the Antelope and left George on the train to come and get us if we didn't hear the helicopter landing. We had to skirt the hump to get to the Antelope pub. All the wagons at the hump end had been moved away and nothing was moving. I had never seen the Mills so quiet. A solitary policeman was stood by the box van. He took a bit of abuse from the gang as they wanted to know who was going to pinch it and, if it blew up, would he come and tell us. As we walked down the road the fire brigade were arriving. They must have been on a call because the fire station is only half a mile away from Temple Mills.

Bert introduced us all to the landlord and I am sure he was getting free drinks for bringing us all into the pub, as well as being in the whip.

Nothing happened whilst we were in there and, as we all left at closing time, we made our way back to the breakdown train acknowledging the policeman who was still there. The helicopter arrived at 2330 and landed on a bit of flat land close to the hump.

I left the lads in the train and went over to it. The R.A.F. officer climbed out and I introduced myself. As we walked over to the box van he told me it had thunder flashes in it. I thought thunder flashes were big fireworks they used in training but, no, these were thunder flash missiles. There were three in long wooden boxes. He thought that they would be safe and we were allowed to re-rail the wagon. The job was completed by 0030 hours and we were back in the shed by 0100 hours.

It was around that time that the empty forty five ton tank arrived for my training exercise with the M.F.D. I thought it would be more of a test of their skills to work on a loaded tank than with an empty one so I started to fill it up with water. It took about three days with just a hose pipe running all the time.

I arranged that the training days would be 10th and 11th September as long as we weren't called out. Inevitably, we were called out on the ninth at 2300 hours to the hump at Temple Mills. An engineer's foundation train had derailed coming down through the retarder. The engineer's foundation train consisted of flat wagons with a ten foot wheel base and on the top of them were large cement mixers. These were used for making the foundations for the overhead gantries. Six wagons were involved. Two were on their side and the other four derailed and tangled together. They were all top heavy and had labels on them stating "not to be hump shunted" in large letters.

Bert made steam while John started cutting them apart. They were all re-railed at 0620 hours and we were clear to return to Stratford at 0730 hours. On our return to the new shed, I had the guard stop the breakdown train with the M.F.D. van opposite the tank we were going to play with.

After a good fry up with food obtained from a milkman I made a start and used the high step jacks with the flat jacking heads to turn over the tank and it crashed to the floor. The ladders were taken out of the train and one of them fitted under the tank to the sole bar, with the top rung of the ladder just above where the top of the jack would be. We changed the heads of the jacks and, because there was no urgency, I could go through the operational procedure with them at leisure. I had the first jack under the top rung of the ladder and it took the weight. The jack was fully extended and the tank hadn't moved. All we did was take out the slack of the wire ladder. The second jack was put in place inside the first and extended. This time the tank started to rotate. The gap between the barrel of the tank and the ground was getting bigger and I had the lads pack it with sleepers and long packing. This was to take away any likelihood of an accident if anything slipped or failed. Because the tank had been rolled off the track, when we started to roll it back the wheel flanges made contact with the rails. It would normally be ideal but, with having steel to steel, there was a possibility that the wheels would turn or slip off the rails. I had the wheels which were touching the track blocked and scotched.

I was glad I had filled the tank with water as it did make it more difficult and the gang was very aware of the weight they were moving. Because the tank was full, its centre of gravity was higher and, when we got it passed the point of balance, the tank would quickly drop onto its wheels. Also, because of its high centre of gravity, it could continue with its roll and go over the opposite way. Packing was placed above the rails where the wheels would land. This would stop the tank from rolling right over.

The use of the M.F.D. went well and I was pleased with the outcome. As we were loading the equipment into the M.F.D. van, Terry, one of the foreman's assistants who call out the gang, came over to us with a telegram telling us to make our way to Ripple Lane. A class 47 had derailed in the West Yard, 47007, and the Ripple Lane gang wanted assistance.

The Ripple Lane breakdown patch was mainly the London, Tilbury and Southend area which ran to Shoeburyness. Their hump had been flattened and they had lost their small crane before I arrived at Stratford. I was told they had a busy gang but the derailments had fallen off and, with the building of the diesel shed, the staffing levels had dropped. Two supervisors shared looking after the breakdown on a part time basis, one was a Carriage and Wagon supervisor, Derek, and the other one was John who worked mainly in the shed on the locos. Whenever Stratford was called to their patch, I would always take whoever was available from Ripple Lane and have them assist us. A couple of the fitter's mates wanted to change sheds and come to Stratford with the hope of getting on the Stratford gang but, when I told them how busy we were, they decided against it as they told me they wanted some sort of social life.

We arrived at the West Yard of Ripple Lane and the loco was re-railed within the hour. We returned to Stratford just before 1900 hours and had a well earned pint in the B.R.S.A club.

Over a few weeks, I had been watching the building of a new retarder at the back of the cattle dock. It was a secondary one and would replace the one in G fan. It was a sixty feet long piece of track, heavier than normal track because of the phosphor bronze rubbing plates and all the pistons that worked them. Finsbury Park breakdown would be bringing their crane over to assist us in the change over. Their crane was the same as ours, a seventy five ton steam crane.

We started early on a Sunday morning with a tandem lift. Removing the retarder from the cattle dock and placing it on a Salmon. The two breakdown trains were then shunted to the hump end of the Mills. Because it was our job I would do the awkward lift. We were sitting on a steep bit of railway at the start of the climb up the hump, with our crane placed above the H fan retarder. The Finsbury Park crane was at the bottom of the G fan retarder, on almost flat track. As the Stratford crane was going to work with a falling gradient behind us, I had an eighteen inch square long balk of timber chained to the track just below the crane. This was to stop the crane if it ran away. As the two cranes were being set up, the O.D.M. was uncoupling the fish plates and all the air and hydraulic pipes which run underground to the retarder. The plan was that we would remove the existing retarder and place it on a Salmon behind our crane. Then have the Salmon shunted away and the new one shunted into place behind us, and while all this shunting was going on we would stop for dinner. I had Sonny, a fitter's mate, in the kitchen preparing the food. Sonny was Albert's brother-in-law and quite an old boy.

I must say it looked a dangerous lift for the Stratford crane as we would be lifting on the low end and side of the crane. I had the lads double pack the outriggers then I slewed the crane round into position. The chains were being fastened onto the retarder when Sonny jumped out of the riding van. He came over to me as white as a sheet and said he wouldn't go back into the riding van on his own because of the ghost. Sliding doors and drawers had opened and shut on their own and poor Sonny couldn't cope with it. Ted said that he didn't mind so he changed jobs with Sonny. He went to make the dinner and Sonny stayed on the floor.

Both cranes took a lift and held the retarder a few inches off the floor whilst the crane packing was checked. We had no movement to the rear wheels or the packing, and there was no need to put the load down. I was jibbing up and slewing to the left while the Finsbury Park crane was slewing right and jibbing out. The load was kept close to the ground until it was alongside the empty Salmon. It was then lifted up and loaded on to the long wagon.

It was time for dinner and Ted had it ready. We all gave Sonny a ribbing about the ghost, but I must admit the riding van did feel cold and it was a hot day outside. Sonny showed us what had happened and which drawers had opened. The funny thing was that the drawers were all full of kitchen utensils and quite heavy to pull open and push shut.

We finished dinner and the new retarder was on the salmon behind our crane. The lads pulled down on the outriggers before we started. The job went well and we soon had the new retarder on the floor where it was wanted. The Finsbury Park gang put their crane away and departed with barely a word spoken between the two gangs. They obviously didn't get on together. It seems that on an earlier tandem lift the Finsbury Park gang had loaded up some of the Stratford packing and a chain with their own, and this caused a bit of a barney. We returned to the cattle dock and off loaded the old retarder. The O.D.M. had cut it into sections so there was very little weight on each lift.

Bill was coming up to retirement and we had a little do for him. Not the shed, just the Breakdown gang, wives and some pals. The obvious place to have it was the B.R.S.A. club. It was a good night and the poor old chap was almost in tears when I presented him with a plaque. On it was a painting of the crane working at the hump, lifting a ferry wagon that had derailed in February. The chap who had done the painting for me was the sign writer. Before he came to work on the railway he was a restorer of war damaged paintings and he was a brilliant artist. The wood for the plaque came from a toilet seat lid. It was the only bit of shiny wood I could find that was wide enough. One of the carpenters in the Out Door Machinery Department did the cutting and carving. None of the women or guests knew where the wood had come from but it tickled Bill when we told him.

With Bill leaving the job I found an eager cockney lad, Kenny, and he lived just by the Mills close to the offices.

We had a quiet day on the 12th, but on the 13th we were called to Ilford where an E.M.U. had derailed. Before we departed we received another call to go to the West end of Temple Mills. The engineer's foundation wagons that had been derailed on the hump were being shunted to the C&W repair road and one had derailed on plain track. We popped it back on and, before we departed to Ilford, another of the wagons jumped off. I thought it may be a good idea to check them all out and I found bent axles on most of them. The breakdown train was on a track between the damaged wagons and the C&W repair road. I decided to crane all the wagons from the road that they stood on to the C&W repair road by lifting them and slewing them over the breakdown train. Then we could depart to Ilford. Again we were thwarted. A loco 37060 had derailed at Stansted blocking the up and down main lines. The loco had been running from the down to the up and split number 10 points. Number one bogie was derailed all wheels and number two bogie had one pair of wheels on the floor. We used the M.F.D. jacks and the up main was clear at 1750 hours and the down was clear at 1805 hours. Trains had been trapped and others backed up behind them so the B.D.V.s were shunted into the sidings until all the trains had been cleared. It was 2000 hours before we could continue to Ilford.

When we arrived at Ilford the Yard Manager said he was thinking of calling the Ripple Lane gang as it had taken us so long to get there. Within a half hour the E.M.U. was re-railed and we adjourned to "The Bell".

From 13th September to the 8th October we were out and about every day or night. Then we had three days without a call and the gang were calling each other to make sure their telephones were working, believing that they were missing calls. One of the rules I made was that if a man missed a call he would have to have a very good reason. If anyone missed two, without covering himself with one of the deputy mates, he needn't bother turning up for the next job and he would be off call.

On 12th October the Mickeldever train made up of empty forty five ton oil tanks had derailed at Grays station on the down road. At 1220 hours the call went out and we arrived in the Grays up sidings at 1500 hours. The loco which pulled our breakdown train, 31003, shunted off the riding van and the crane with Bert and Ted on the footplate. They drove the crane along the Up road towards the wreckage.

Eight tanks had become derailed of which one was on the platform on its side, and another was also on its side up against the signal box. Two more had lost both sets of wheels. The job was in Ripple Lane's patch and their supervisor, Derek, was going to walk back along the track to look for anything which may have caused the accident whilst I got on with the re-railing.

If I remember correctly, it was a Wednesday lunch time and half day closing at Grays when the derailment happened. On any other day of the week the platform would have been full of people who would have been mown down by the tank as it slid along over half of the length of the platform. Another tank impacted on the signal box giving the signalmen the fright of their lives as they believed the box was going to crash to the ground. Not one person was injured in the whole derailment. I soon realised that I was going to have problems removing the tanks from site as four of them had wheels missing or were badly damaged and I only had the one emergency bogie.

We re-railed the four that were upright and then I had some of the gang find some wooden sleepers or stout timbers and lay them across the buffers of the tanks we had re-railed. I then lifted a tank without wheels and rested its buffers on top of the timber resting on the runnable tank buffers. I did this at both ends of the badly damaged tank. This way of recovering a vehicle is called piggy backing. I used some of the tanks that hadn't been derailed as they hadn't been removed from site. All this took a good deal of time.

The fire brigade were in attendance all the time we were there and the fire chief told me that the lads couldn't smoke on site. As he was telling me this, the flame coming out of the crane chimney was about two foot high. When I pointed this out to him he told me he couldn't do anything about that but he could do something about us smoking. He showed me a meter which could determine if explosive gas was in the area and a reading near the lid of one of the tanks which was on its side was high. The tanks were all empty of petrol and hadn't been purged so any fumes that escaped would have been highly explosive. After that anyone who wanted a quick smoke would climb on to the crane footplate and light up.

The water was getting low in the crane water tanks and Bert was starting to worry so I saw the fire chief and had one of the fire engines fill up the tanks.

The local W.V.S. had set up a tea and coffee counter with sandwiches by the station ticket office and were handing out refreshments to the lads. By 0315 hours I had two strings of tanks sitting on the rails or on top of other tanks and I started to move them at walking pace into Tilbury Wall Sidings. I had to tie the tanks together with chains and pull lifts to stop them falling apart on the half mile we had to walk them.

It was 0700 hours when we eventually cleared the up and down main lines and 1015 when the B.D.V.s were ready to depart to Stratford. I went to see the Bobby in the box. He had recovered from his ordeal the day before and told me we were wanted back at Temple Mills to clear two small derailments. We departed Grays at 1030 hours and we all slept until we arrived at the Mills at 1545 hours. With a good five hours sleep and a mug of tea we were ready for the two quick jobs. A hopper off all wheels in G fan and three wagons in A fan derailed and lock buffered. By 1800 hours we were back in the shed and, as we all had slept well, we went to the B.R.S.A. club.

On 15th October at 2130 hours we went back to Grays and the sidings at Tilbury to load up the four tanks that couldn't run, and were back at Stratford 1700 hours the next day.

The firemen were threatening to go on strike in November and I was told by management that, because I was in charge of the emergencies on the railway, I was to come up with an idea in case we were involved with a fire in or around the shed. We had much better rescue equipment than the fire brigade if anything happened to a passenger train, so we had no worries about that. The only worrying thing was fire.

The O.D.M. had a small lorry with a box on the back. I thought that it might be ideal. I had it loaded with water and powder fire extinguishers, bags of sand and axes. All firemen carry axes. The lorry would be driven by the O.D.M. driver who always drove it whilst he was on shift but after he had gone home it would be down to me. I tried starting it up one night and the battery was flat. The next day I had the O.D.M. fit a charger in the new shed so that the lorry could be left on trickle charge all night. Luckily we were never called to use it, but it was there ready.

9th September, 1977. Cement mixer on foundation train with
broken axle.

Removing canopy off ADB966111 using 45 ton steamer.
19th February, 1977.

Between 15th October and 11th November we had twenty three small local derailments and on the 11th we were called to Angel Road. A guards brake van B951773 and two wagons were on their side. Using the forty five ton crane all the wagons were re-railed within two hours.

From 12th November to the 28th we only had ten calls to Temple Mills, Leyton and Ilford. On the 28th we were called to Bow Depot. Fifteen loaded oil tanks had run away and impacted on the buffer stops at the bottom of a sloping road. The tank which had hit the stops, ALG49100, had demolished the stops and travelled thirty feet, then sunk in the dirt up to its buffers. It took longer than normal because we had to dig it out. I wanted it off loading to make it lighter and safer but there was no pump or empty tank available. I had the remaining tanks pulled off so we had room for the tank but, with no adjacent road to sit the crane on, we had to use the M.F.D. jacks and, because of the packing sinking so quickly into the dirt, I damaged three sets of pipes before we had it re-railed over four hours later.

On 1st December, Bert went to March to bring back our seventy five ton crane. It was en route from the works and had to have a rider with it. A rider, usually a crane driver or someone who knows the crane well, is needed to repeatedly check on the crane, on the springs and hanger bolts and to check the running gear, also the outriggers, to make sure the retaining pins are still in place. An accident has sometimes been caused by an outrigger sliding out whilst a crane was being hauled along the track into the path of an oncoming train or striking track furniture or a platform. Bert left it in Temple Mills late on the 2nd to be picked up the next day by the trip loco and I would go with the loco to bring it to the shed.

While Bert was bringing our crane back, we had four calls to the Mills. The first was at 0025 hours with a follow on and the third at 1100 hours with another follow on, but we had finished at 1330 hours.

The next day I ran down to the Mills with the trip loco and the crane stood resplendent on its own in the cattle dock road. I had forgotten just how big our seventy five ton crane was. It had been painted yellow and looked very different from the crane that had gone away all those months ago. The boiler and water tanks had gone and in their place on the back was a long compartment with the diesel engine in it. A proper cab had been built so the driver wouldn't be bothered by the weather but he still couldn't see anything. Instead of the pistons on the side just in front of the cab were hydraulic motors.

I would have a great deal of trouble with this crane in the following months but the report I received back from the main works was pleasing. They said that it was the most well looked after crane they had seen and they hadn't needed to do any riveting. Not like the one from the north of the country which had to be taken to a ship yard for re-riveting. Derby works had done away with riveters as a consequence of the demise of steam.

The loco driver and yard shunters were tying the crane to the loco and I went to see the Yard Manager to get the crane released to me. We took the crane back to the new shed and put it to one side. I wanted to check it all out before putting it in the train. It looked fine and Bert was running it up when we were called to Channelsea. A loco 37084 had derailed all wheels and was blocking the sidings. We arrived at 1450 hours and I found the cause was the state of the track. All the sleepers were rotten underneath but looked good above the ballast. The rail chair bolts had all moved outwards and the track had spread. The loco looked a sorry sight. As the wheels had hit the sleepers they were all chopped into fire wood and the loco was buried almost up to its buffers.

I couldn't get the forty five ton crane into position as it would mean blocking the up and down main. We had to get out the M.F.D. jacks and most of the packing. We eventually lifted one end up and put good wooden packing under the wheels. I didn't think of pulling the rails into gauge under the wheels one bogie at a time. I thought we could tie the rails together when both bogies were out of the dirt and the rails free to be worked on. It took us just over three hours before we had all the wheels on the rails and then John gently drove it off the damaged track and into the sidings.

Once the loco was clear of the damaged track it was screwed down and trapped in the sidings until the P Way could repair the damage. The loco couldn't be used in traffic as I had arranged for it to be lifted off its bogies and thoroughly examined. As we were putting all the equipment back on the tool vans I noticed we had used over a dozen tie bars to hold the track together.

On the 14th we were called to Tilbury Riverside. Three loaded grain hoppers had derailed and were over on their sides. I thought it sounded like a good job for the little crane. When we arrived no overhead wires had been touched or gantries hit. I asked for the wires to be slewed but was told it would take such a long time we would be there for days. As the gang had recently trained with the ladder jacks at re-righting, that was what we used and within two hours all three were back on the track. We assisted the C&W to fit new axle box guides to B885354 and had a good lunch.

On 20th December, when everyone was looking forward to Christmas, we had three calls early in the morning, mainly derailed coal hoppers.

In the afternoon we did some training with our dieselised crane. This crane was going to be something really different. I could have the crane start up straight away and not have to worry about coal or water. We found that the Detroit diesel was a bit noisy but this had been taken into account and a radio was supplied for communication. I could talk to the crane driver but he had to reply through a public address system fitted under the jib. It was designed like that because, when I gave the driver an instruction, he would repeat it before carrying it out. If I said, "Slew to the right", he would answer, "Slewing to the right" and carry out the movement. All the gang would hear this and know what was going to happen, even the lads on the non-lifting side. Another handy thing was the lighting. The old way was with a steam generator and it was far too noisy. On this crane the generator was powered by the diesel engine and had much more and better lighting. The next day I looked through all the paper work that had come with the crane.

The 22nd December was the busiest day of the year with seven calls, one after the other. We had had four or five in a day but never seven. Most of the calls were in Temple Mills and one at Bow Midland. The fitter, John, was on annual leave for two weeks immediately before Christmas and Dave covered for him on twelve calls. We had just three calls between Christmas and the New Year but were on call the whole time.

This may be a good time to explain how a breakdown man needed an understanding wife and family. If we ever made plans at home to do something, we always had to come up with a plan B., as there was a good likelihood that we wouldn't be available for the family because of a call.

10th September, 1977, outside the new shed used for training.

10th September, 1977, with main offices behind training tank.

CHAPTER 10
1978

We dealt with two hundred and ninety nine derailments in 1978, and twenty three of them were in January.

Up to 9th January we only had three calls but on the 10th at 0325 hours we were called to Ripple Lane. Five loaded fuel oil tanks, two of which were one hundred ton, had derailed and spread over three roads.

Because the fire brigade were still on strike, the R.A.F. and army had turned up with their fire engines. The R.A.F. had a foam nozzle on the top of their fire tender and were covering everything in soap suds. The army had a large blower in a box that produced foam and had set up on the opposite side to the R.A.F. and were blowing soap suds all over that side of the wreckage.

On arrival I asked if any of the tanks were leaking, but the armed forces couldn't say. I couldn't see what the condition of the track was like as it was waist high in foam. I decided to have the two one hundred ton tanks off loaded. This required getting staff from Shell Haven with pumps and two empty tanks to put the fuel oil into. All this was ready by 0930 hours and it took five hours to off load both tanks. The C&W checked for leaks and none were found so I had the forty five ton steam crane run into position and we started re-railing. Both the R.A.F. and the army with their Green Goddesses stood by whilst we completed the job.

As a matter of interest, one of my uncles who worked for the government was involved with the design of the Green Goddesses.

The last tank was re-railed at 1830 hours and we started to put everything away ready to depart. The R.A.F. and army said their goodbyes and departed. With all the soap suds covering everything, all the equipment that had come into contact with it was spotlessly clean.

Most of the calls we had in January were grain hoppers or tanks. On 20th January a Class 47, 47014 was derailed in the Freight Liner Terminus at Stratford. We went from there to the Mills. Two mineral wagons were derailed and lock buffered.

On our return to the shed I was going to give the diesel crane the last once over before I had it put in the train. I smelled something I didn't want to. I followed the smell and traced it to one of the main bearings on the drive shaft. As soon as I put my hand on it I knew I had problems because it was very hot. I rang the works at Derby and told them the problem and mentioned that I hadn't put the crane in the train as yet. They told me that they would dispatch a pair of fitters to sort it out. The fitters would be with us on the 24th.

Before they arrived we were called to Leyton Depot at 0030 hours on the 22nd. A tamper had derailed all wheels at a set of points. Tampers are quite heavy but very flimsy. They are used to fluff up the ballast under the track. Hydraulic arms are thumped down either side of a sleeper end into the ballast. They close slightly and do a short lift. They release and thump down again, close and lift. Then do it all again quite quickly. This action moves the ballast about under the sleepers so that it doesn't get solid and have no give in it.

On 24th January we had just returned from re-railing a mineral wagon in Temple Mills and met the fitters from Derby. We set up the forty five ton crane next to the seventy five tonner and used it to remove the long canopy from the top of the diesel crane and then the jib gear box. The fitters had brought with them new bearings and some special grease and had hoped to finish the job in a day, but ended up staying in a B&B on the Romford Road.

26th January the fitters had gone back to Derby, promising to return with others as the job was bigger than they first thought.

The crane was just two hundred tons of scrap at that time. We would have to manage with the little forty five ton steam crane.

Early that day we were called to Thames Haven. A loco, 37049 had derailed all wheels number one bogie. Whilst we were re-railing it a shunter from the yard asked if we could re-rail a guards van B955143 and a barrier wagon B748136 that had been pushed over the buffer stops at the end of a shunting spur. The guards van and the wagon had been there for a couple of weeks and no one in the yard would take responsibility for the derailment. I said that we would and moved our train to the end of the yard by the shunting spur. It was bitterly cold as we started to re-rail the offending vehicles and it started to sleet. I looked over a wall and we were less than fifty feet from the sea. There was a right gale blowing off the sea and the tops of the waves were being blown straight towards us. It was grand to climb back into the warm riding van and make our way back inland.

The Derby fitters returned on the 30th with extra staff and equipment and started to repair and re-build the diesel crane. The next day, the 31st, I couldn't help them because we were called to Temple Mills. We used the steam crane on three wagons B745934, B745110 and B745237 in D fan. We then went to the Manor sidings to re-rail a match wagon B462770.

On our return to the shed the works staff were preparing to leave after telling me the crane was now fully operational.

On 1st February I put the diesel crane on the back of the train and we went to A fan in Temple Mills. Five loaded grain hoppers were derailed and tangled together. We used the repaired crane and it worked as it should. After re-railing two mineral wagons in H fan we returned to the shed and refitted the canopy to the diesel crane using the little steam crane to lift it up. I then had the diesel crane put in the train.

2nd February in the early evening a call came for us to go to Bow Midland. 31255 had derailed number one bogie. I mention this one because we used ramps to re-rail it. Because the track was so badly damaged and the wheels of the derailed bogie were sitting up high and not dropped down into the dirt, ramps seemed the ideal way to get the loco back on to the track. Ramps are only used when the track or loco wont be damaged. With the ramps set close to the leading wheels and good packing in front of the second and third wheels the loco was gently pulled up the ramp. As it was on top of the ramp I stopped the loco pulling and had more packing placed in the gaps left by the wheels. With a slow pull all the wheels ran along the packing and on to the ramp and then onto the track. The whole job took twenty minutes. Using ramps incorrectly can damage the track or traction motors on the loco but, if the track is already beyond repair and the loco wheels are sitting on the sleeper chairs and high enough to pack so that they will roll freely and not damage the traction motors, a loco can be re-railed this way.

February was a busy month at times and I used the big diesel crane on many occasions. We were watching the bearings closely and on the 10th we smelled the bearings running hot again. As I was so disillusioned with the work that had been carried out by Derby Works, I had the crane sent back to them to do the work correctly. This time I would go there myself to see it on test and make sure everything was bedded in as it should be after the work was finished.

I had been asked to form a blue asbestos gang because more people were talking about it on the railway and in the press. I used the lads on the breakdown as they all knew the equipment and how to use it. I had a storage room built in the new shed with a small office at one side. It was for all the equipment to be used in asbestos conditions. On one wall there was a row of battery chargers so that all the power packs which ran the air pumps we all had to carry on a belt were always ready to be used.

One of the first jobs we were involved in with asbestos was the lift shaft at Norton Folgate. Norton Folgate was a large stores for C&W equipment and was on three floors just outside Liverpool Street Station. The lift shaft was coated with asbestos and the workers knew this and threatened to stop work if nothing was done.

On 11th February, I think it was a Sunday, I took John and Ray to Norton Folgate to cover the asbestos with a special paint. The paint had wonderful properties and was very expensive. When built up in layers the paint would dry but be elastic. Another thing was that it was fire proof.

We had just arrived to spray the lift shaft at Norton Folgate when we were given a message to go to Goodmayes. A motorail train 4G71 had three vehicles derailed at catch points. John, Ray and myself went to site by road and met the train at Goodmayes. We used the M.F.D. to re-rail the empty vehicles and returned to Stratford. We didn't have time to go back to Norton Folgate and spray paint the lift shaft. It was arranged that we would return on another Sunday.

We dealt with seven calls that week and on Saturday on the second call as we were using the crane to sort out a load of hoppers Bert told me that he was losing steam. As it was taking such a long time to complete a move it was 2200 hours before we were finished. The next day I arranged for the boiler to be washed out again. I had the O.D.M. give the crane a general examination. We were using the crane so often that the tubes were sooting up.

The month of March arrived in which we had thirty two calls. On 6th March at 2310, our third job was back at the Klondike sidings at Southend. A four car E.M.U. had derailed in six road. Whilst we were waiting for the isolation, I looked for the cause of the derailment and found a wooden key in the points. It had dropped in or been placed by someone between the point blades. The wooden keys are placed in the gap between the rail and the sleeper chairs and hammered home to hold the rail firmly in place. It was probably vandalism but I couldn't prove it. The isolation was implemented at 0300 hours and we used the M.F.D. to re-rail the coaches. We were back in the shed at Stratford by 0600 hours.

On 8th March we were re-railing a shunting loco 08724 that had come off all wheels in the Mills and found one of the crane springs had broken. Luckily six spare springs were delivered with the crane and we changed the broken one before returning to the shed.

I was told the seventy five ton diesel crane was ready for me to look at in Derby Works. I arranged to go up on the 10th and stay the night. This would give me two days to check it thoroughly. When I arrived it was on the test bed. I had them lift weights of different tonnage and slew them round. I had the crane working for a good five hours and found nothing amiss. I told the staff I would want to do the same again the next day and went to the railway school where I was staying the night. The next day I was on their backs all morning and I had them slewing and derricking all the time. At midday I told them I was satisfied with the crane and we all went for lunch. On the way I was taken into a part of the works where work was going on re-building riding vans and to my horror there was one with Stratford on the side. I needed a new riding van, but this one was a riding/packing van with less room for the lads as half the van was used for packing and equipment. I told them they could send it to a small gang who would benefit from having it. With that parting comment, I came home hoping the crane would soon follow.

On the 14th we didn't get a call until 1130 hours to Mile End. Loco 37260 had derailed all wheels number two bogie. We popped it on within twenty minutes of arriving and set off to Temple Mills. Two mineral wagons were waiting for us. On arrival at the Mills I saw that the diesel crane had been brought back from the works. I had the crane shunted on to the back of the train and we took it back with us to the shed.

We were so busy that I didn't have time to put the diesel crane in the train until the 18th when we went to March Lane to load up new wheel sets to fit to the tanks that had been left at Grays. The following day we left the shed at 0700 hours and the wheels were fitted by 1200 hours. We were told that there was a possession on at Barking and we wouldn't get a path until it was given up at 1800 hours. The crane had worked well and I thought all the problems with it were finished. I hoped I could be rid of the forty five ton steam crane.

On the 21st we were on standby for a royal from 2000 hours to 2300 hours, and it was uneventful. As soon as we should have stood down we were told a mineral wagon was in the Manor Yard waiting to be re-railed.

I had been promised a new riding van, but had not liked the one I had seen at Derby. The saloon part was more like a passenger coach with sets of four seats around small tables. I could see the gang splitting up into groups and wanted to keep them as a total unit. Also on the new van I wanted beds and a shower for the lads. Worst of all was the size of my office, which was too small. I had been working on some plans of the van I wanted. I quickly finished them off and had them sent to the Regional Manager who promised me that they would be forwarded.

On 6th April we were called to Chadwell Heath. The 0146 departure, Temple Mills to Ipswich, had three bogie bolsters derailed blocking the down main. I was asked to wait for a C&W inspector. I waited for twenty minutes but he never arrived so I had the guard get us away. The three bogie bolsters ADM123863, ADM107884 and ADM127806 were the rear three of ten wagons and all were empty.

I found a retaining chain in the points, 101B, which controlled the up electric to the down main. It looked as if it had come off ADM123863 and had wedged in the points causing the derailment. As the wagons were low Salmons I didn't need an isolation and because they were light they hadn't damaged any of the track, so we speedily re-railed them with the M.F.D. equipment. With the breakdown train standing on the up road and the lads working from the M.F.D. van it took just one and a half hours to clear the site.

I have mentioned some of the wagons by name. It may be a good time to explain to non-railway readers how the names came about for the infrastructure wagons. One of the earlier managers on the railway was a fisherman. He named all the wagons after fish or sea creatures. The names usually corresponded with the size or shape of the fish. The smallest wagon I ever saw was a Periwinkle. It was a very short low open wagon and there were not many of them about.

The biggest and heaviest is the Whale. The Whale is a hundred ton hopper and is used to carry ballast to engineering sites. There are chutes under the wagons for off loading the ballast. The doors to the chutes are opened by one of three big wheels on the end of the wagons. The wheels on the left and right correspond to the chutes on that particular side. The middle one opens the chute to drop the ballast between the rails. Smaller hoppers are called Sea Cows and Sea Lions. I say smaller but they are still over fifty tons when loaded. If ballast was to be dropped from the middle chute, a Shark Brake would be marshalled somewhere in the train. The Shark is a guards' brake with two heavy ploughs underneath pointing to either end. The plough is shaped like a proper plough but has gaps where it sits on the track when it is lowered. A big wheel, not unlike a ships steering wheel, is positioned at either end inside the open section of the brake. As the wheel is turned the plough drops down. When the train is moved over the dropped ballast the plough pushes the high mounds of ballast. The excess is ploughed to the sides or pushed into hollows. I think it is called a Shark because the plough looks like a shark's mouth when it is screwed up under the brake. The smaller of the ballast wagons were Mermaids. These were side tipping wagons with low sides.

Other wagons are called Clams. These are short mineral wagons and vacuum braked. The corresponding air braked wagon is a Rudd. The Clams and Rudd have metal sides. There is Bass which is half as long again as the Rudd. They have middle doors that drop down and are mostly wooden sided. Then there is another

12th October, 1977.

22nd January, 1978, Tamper off all wheels.

group of wagons longer than the Bass but with lower sides. These are called Seahorse, Seahare, and Sea Urchin and they are all very similar. The longer wagons which are about sixty feet in length are called Salmons. These are bogie vehicles and flat topped for carrying sections of made up track. Five sections can be loaded on top of each other and they have to be chained down correctly. A load examiner has to verify that they are fit to travel and place load examined cards on either side of the wagon. Another type of Salmon is the bogie bolster. Instead of a flat top it has bolsters positioned crossways along the top. These wagons are for carrying sections of rail or long bits of steel. In each bolster are pockets which take three feet high cast iron pins to stop the rails from rolling off the side. This is another job for the load examiner. Another Salmon type vehicle with a non fish name is the Bedstead. It is a bogie bolster but has high ends that look like bed heads and a canopy along the top held up with strong steel pillars. This makes it look something like a four poster bed. This wagon has two fixed diesel cranes fitted to one side with the jibs over the carrying area. The jibs extend about a foot. Rails can be loaded or off loaded at site using the two jibs. If the diesel oil has run out or the motors have packed in, there is a handle on each jib to operate everything. A Tench is a sixty foot bogie wagon with low wooden sides. It's lower than a normal Salmon because it has smaller wheels. It is usually used for moving signal posts and gantries or other long engineers equipment. If the load doesn't overhang the sides or stick up too high it isn't required to be load examined.

The problem with all these wagons used to be that they had oil axle boxes. They had to be examined on every trip and have the oil level topped up. Some would get missed and occasionally would run hot, sometimes with disastrous results. It would take many years before all these wagons were fitted with roller bearings.

On the 6th, 7th, and 8th April we had the jib up in the Mills. The first two days we had shunting locos off, 08269 and 08552. On the third day we re-railed a string of mineral wagons. The crane was behaving itself and it was a pleasure to use.

On 11th April we had three calls to the hump. These were only miner derailments, one or two wagons each time. The cause for all of them was ice and snow building up on the retarder.

The second call on the 13th was to the buffer stops on the shunting spur in the West Yard. The driver on 31148 had misread a signal and instead of powering his light engine on to the main line, he ran full tilt into the stops. The stops had often been demolished so the P Way had built much sturdier ones and set them in foundations of concrete. As the loco impacted on the stops, instead of them braking, they were pushed forwards and down. The concrete foundation came up out of the ground and the underneath of the loco caught it and rolled it forward. When we arrived, the front end of the loco was high in the air being held up by an eight foot square lump of concrete. Behind the concrete was the hole that it had come out of. The hole was the same size as the lump of concrete and the second bogie had almost dropped into it. The driver and second man were unable to climb out of the leading cab as it was too high. They had to walk through the engine room at a steep angle and exit the loco by the rear cab.

By standing the big crane on the road the driver thought that he was taking, we re-railed the rear bogie first. We had great difficulty fitting the lifting brackets to the high end of the loco. Firstly, we were unable to reach the pockets that the brackets fitted into and, secondly, the pockets were at an angle. The first problem was dealt with by building up packing on both sides. The packing had to be wide enough for four men to stand on and with iron bars and brute strength the second problem was solved. With the crane well bedded down we took a lift and 31148 rose up off the concrete block. We had disconnected the brake work on the rear bogie so it would run along the track when we slewed the crane to the right. Everything was going smoothly then Bert shouted over the tannoy that a low hydraulic oil warning light had come on. I had all the staff stand out of the way of any danger in case the load dropped and I quickly slewed the crane and had Bert lower the block. There is a fail safe brake on the main drive shaft that should hold everything if there is a loss of hydraulic oil pressure, but I didn't like to rely on it too much.

The loco was badly damaged at the front and underneath with the leading bogie in a right mess. It took a while to get the loco back into gauge in order for it to be hauled back to the shed. There was only a small section of main line to travel over but I didn't want the damaged loco to foul anything running on the adjacent roads. Whilst we were putting the jib down one of the lads spotted a broken spring on the crane. That had to be changed before we could go back to the shed. I had a loco come out of the shed to drag 31148 back and we followed it in case the damaged bogie caused it to come off again.

I tried to get the gang stood down for the 14th. Bill had passed away and his funeral was to be in the afternoon. I was told that no way would they allow the gang to be stood down in order to go to a funeral but I may release two of the gang to go. Ted and Kevin were the two who represented us. It was barely six months since Bill had retired and it was a common thing to happen to railway men who had just finished work. They would be working long shifts all the time, both day and night, and that was all they knew. As soon as they stopped work they seemed to go down hill fast.

In May we dealt with thirty calls, four of which were on the 12th. The first was at 0600 hours. Two wagons loaded with scrap had derailed and were blocking B fan. The crane was set up and we were going to take the first lift when we heard a continuous rumble of bangs coming from the main line. A string of mixed wagons being pulled by 08554 had become derailed blocking both up and down main lines. I had the gang put away the crane because I knew we would have to deal with the blocked main line first. I went over to see the driver on the 08 who was on a line side telephone arguing with the Bobby in the signal box. The driver thought the road hadn't been set properly and the signalman thought that the train was going too fast. I talked with the driver and he told me that he was only travelling at fifteen m.p.h. and this was backed up by the second man. Also, the signalman had asked the driver to move his string of wagons as quickly as possible off the main. I knew everything would have to be put on paper back at the shed. I had them take their bags off the loco and make their way back to fill in all the reports, then I went to see the signalman.

The Bobby was in a bit of a state and very excitable. I had him make a pot of tea and, after he calmed down, he told me his version of the facts. He told me that he had asked the driver to be as quick as possible because he had a train standing at a signal waiting to go through his patch. He showed me his points and how they were set. I made sure the site was protected and filled in the log accordingly. A signal inspector arrived to check up on the Bobby and I arranged with him where I would put the breakdown train to clear the wagons. The dispute with the driver and the Bobby would not be resolved until I had examined the wagons. Our guard, Martin, had come over to the box and asked me where I wanted the train to be stopped.

I checked the derailed wagons and initially it looked a mess. There were long wheel base wagons in between short wheel base wagons and all had green cards or one trip only cards on them. The train was a load of wagons going for repairs. All the wagons were empty which made re-railing a lot easier. Six in all had to be re-railed. I had John, George and Albert start with hand jacks on the wagons close to the track and I used the rest of the lads with the M.F.D. Within forty minutes all the wheels were back on the track and we moved them clear of the main line and into one of the reception roads. I checked the wagons with John and found the cause.

One of the ferry wagons B787380 had a spring hanger broken which resulted in a light axle. The weight of the wagon wasn't being held up at that corner and the buffer had dropped and was lower than is allowed. With that and having a short wheel base wagon coupled to it the result was a buffer lock which pushed the small wagon to one side and a wheel struck a check rail resulting in the six wagons coming off. I informed the signal inspector that the signalman was clear of any blame. The derailment was a mechanical fault. I also rang the Operation's Manager and told him the same story and that the driver was in the clear.

We returned to B fan and re-railed the two scrap wagons. With another two follow on calls we were still finished before the B.R.S.A. shut at lunch time.

On 17th May the third job was a Paxman shunting loco A.D.B. 968001. The Paxman was built to look a little bit like a steam loco. The exhaust came out of a long funnel at the front. It was a diesel hydraulic and only half the size of an 08 shunting loco. The reason for this derailment was the thin flanges on the tyres. They had split the facing points and dropped onto the ballast.

We finished May with thirty calls.

In June we had twenty seven jobs. On 6th June the third call that day was to Stanford le Hope. The second coach of a four car E.M.U. E61122 had derailed just the one pair of wheels. What had happened was that the tyre on the right hand side wheel had come adrift and caused the derailment. All the loco and C&W fitters will know about the tyres on the wheels. Just to explain what they are. The tyres are made of much harder steel than the wheel and they carry the profile of the flange that keeps the wheel on the rails. The tyres are held on to the wheel by a Gibson ring on the inside of the wheel. Older people may remember the long hammer man who would walk on the ballast alongside a train in a platform, usually at the bigger stations, and tap the tyres of every wheel. If anyone was looking out of a window they would hear the ring as he tapped the wheel. This indicated that the tyre was tight and had no cracks in it. If it didn't ring, the coach would have to be knocked out of the train for further examination.

If I may digress a little. Thinking about the long hammer man or wheel tapper, reminds me of the communication cord in all the passenger coaches. It ran the full length of the carriage through a conduit above the windows. It was connected to a valve at the end of the carriage. This valve was spring loaded and the slightest tug would operate the valve opening the vacuum or air brake pipe to the atmosphere. It didn't give a full brake application but indicated to the driver a partial loss of vacuum or drop on the air. The driver would bring the train safely to a stand at a position of his choosing. Though most of the times a communication cord is pulled it's a false alarm, the driver has to get the train into a position where it can be evacuated if need be. Not in a tunnel nor on a bridge or viaduct. The reason I remembered it is the butterfly on the valve on the end of the coach. The butterfly is a piece of metal shaped like a three inch long flag usually painted white and when the cord is pulled it turns down to indicate in which coach the cord has been pulled. The long hammer man was supposed to check that all the butterflies were horizontal as he walked along the train. All the guard had to do to reset the valve was turn the butterfly horizontal and the driver would get his full brake.

On 14th June we started at 0030 hours and went to Shenfield station. The 2200 X Ipswich to Temple Mills was blocking the up main with a dropped axle on the tenth vehicle DB990633. It was the result of a hot box. One of the journal end's of the axle had burned off and, luckily, it hadn't derailed. On arrival we built up the emergency bogie under the wagon and tied up the offending axle. Whilst we were doing this the other wagons at the front and back were shunted away from DB990633 with the loco 31244. The rest of the train continued to Temple Mills. Within forty minutes of arriving we were pushing the wagon on the emergency bogie into the sidings by number one platform.

Later that day we were reloading a wagon B923348. The load had moved in a rough shunt. We were using the diesel crane and it started playing up. The cant indicator was showing a hundred millimetres, or six inches. This was wrong as I knew we were on good flat track. The high low and over end alarms were sounding

24th June, 1978, at Dagenham Dock.

for no apparent reason. Bert was having a bad time with all the different alarms going off. We managed to cancel them and finish the reloading.

Back at the shed that afternoon and the next day, I was working with an electrician from the O.D.M. who was good at fault finding. The only thing we could find wrong with the crane was that rain had managed to get into one of the corner emergency buttons on the carriage and was shorting out some of the circuits. The emergency mushroom buttons on the corners of the crane carriage were new to the diesel crane and there to be used by members of the gang to warn the driver of rear wheel lift. The electrician who had been working on it for two days told me he had repaired it on the second afternoon whilst we were on stand by for a royal train.

We returned to Shenfield on 18th June to recover our emergency bogie and fit a new pair of wheels under wagon DB000635.

At 1110 hours on the 21st we were called to Ilford Car Sheds. The London end entrance was blocked. A Grampus DB986876 was derailed and a Sturgeon DE470802 was derailed with an overhead gantry across it and another Sturgeon DB994100 and Dolphin DB994035 were derailed and tangled together.

With two gantries down and four large wagons across the yard, Ilford Car Sheds had come to a stop as far as movements were concerned. I found the cause to be two of the wagons getting lock buffered as the train snaked over tight bends into the yard.

I had the breakdown train re-marshalled with the crane leading and ran it off the vans into the centre of the wreckage. The isolation of the overhead line equipment was put on at 1400, though most of the wires were on the floor. The crane worked well and I put the two gantries to one side and re-railed the four wagons. I then assisted the overhead men to assemble two new gantries. I gave my C form or permit to work back at 1710 hours. It had taken us just over three hours to complete the job. The crane jib was down and the guard was re-marshalling our train.

Our loco 31275 was pulling our riding van to place it on the country end of the crane. The loco and riding van ran through a set of points that had been clipped out of use by the Yard Supervisor to protect the derailment site. Unfortunately, the points were damaged by the loco forcing them open and the loco then set back, pushing the riding van through the damaged points and it ended up on the floor. With the crane sitting in the middle of the yard, the two tool vans at the London end of the yard and the loco with the derailed riding van at the country end we were in a right mess. In order to sort it out we had to put some hand jacks on a P Way trolley and push them all the way through the yard. Everyone except for the breakdown gang thought it funny. Our riding van was re-railed at 1800 hours and the points were clipped in the correct direction for the loco and riding van to proceed. We had had a harrowing day and we all adjourned to "The Bell" with instructions to the guard that if he put anything on the floor again he would have to re-rail it himself. We arrived back at the shed at 2030 hours.

On 23rd June we were called to a reloading job. Ten wagons had been involved in a rough shunt, or perhaps they may have come over the hump in a string and collided with a stationary train. Nothing was derailed but all ten had to be reloaded. The crane was working all day. We started at 0700 and finished at 1830 hours.

The next day we had three calls; the first in Temple Mills where two shunting movements came together on converging roads with strings of tanks and hoppers trying to get onto the same bit of track. As they were all empty, I had the crane set up and we could reach all the derailed vehicles without moving.

We departed to Dagenham Dock for the second job where an articulated car transporter had impacted on a car loading ramp and jumped on top of the ramp leaving a bogie behind. We used the crane again but while we were putting it away we found a broken spring on the crane and that had to be changed before we went to Thornton Fields where a motor coach of an E.M.U. had derailed and blocked the entrance. It was spread over several roads. We used the M.F.D equipment because getting the wires moved to use the crane would have taken a long time and, with the yard blocked to coaching stock and E.M.Us, the railway wanted it open again as quickly as possible. We spent all night there, finishing at 0530 hours.

We were in the Mills every day until the end of the month. In July we only had twenty calls locally but we had trouble with the nitrogen on the crane. The nitrogen was used to assist with the movement of the dogs and gave extra pressure to move the dogs across and mesh with the required gear.

August was a quiet month with only twenty three calls. The first one was on the 1st. We were asked to help the Colchester breakdown to re-rail an E.M.U. on the washer road at Clacton on Sea. We departed Stratford at 2300 hours and arrived alongside the washer road three hours later. The overhead wires were switched off but not moved as I had requested. We used the crane and by 0410 hours the job was finished. It would have been much quicker if the wires had been slewed well out of the way. Whilst we were on site I didn't see any of the Colchester gang we were supposed to be helping, just a supervisor.

On 3rd August we were out all night again at Thornton Fields. The call was at 2300 hours. A loco 37049 was derailed all wheels both bogies with a B.S.O. E9369 derailed and trying to climb on to the back cab. The derailment was blocking roads eleven to thirty five. All the track and points were very badly damaged and, again, the overhead wires were still intact. With such a lot of wires above the wreckage, there was no way I could get them all moved so that I could use the crane. We used the M.F.D power jacks and I returned my C form at 0410 hours. The loco was badly damaged and the B.S.O. (Brake Second Class Open) had a bent axle. We departed leaving a great deal of work for the P Way.

I was training Ken on the diesel crane and on 7th August after re-railing four Grampus wagons, he put it away. He was very careful and a little slow but he did what was asked of him. As we departed

Leyton after re-railing the grampus wagons, the jib runner and the riding van became lock buffered on a tight bend. We soon had them parted but the buffers on the riding van were badly bent. As the riding van was so old I knew I wouldn't get new buffers for it. The buffer head had a four feet long spindle that slid into the buffer's body and was held in place with a big nut behind the buffer beam. As soon as I berthed the train I took them to the Diesel Repair Shop and had them straightened.

Ken was doing part of the driving along with Ted and Bert and was coming along nicely.

On 12th August we were called to South Minster where a loaded sand hopper B439505 was derailed all wheels. It was a good run to South Minster and as soon as we arrived I checked the springs and found one had broken. We were using the crane frequently and I thought that all my problems with the crane were over.

On 21st August we had a call to Plaistow. A guards brake van B954792 and loaded coal wagon B271965 were derailed at a set of points to the sidings. When we arrived we couldn't get to the site without blocking the main line so we were stood off in a loop and had to take the equipment we wanted on a plate layer's trolley which we carried on the train. I had checked what equipment we would need and, whilst I was looking at the job, I found that something had been placed in the points and, as children had been seen in the area trespassing, I was pretty sure that they were to blame.

On 23rd August I had the diesel crane shunted out of the train for the Derby fitters to check on the fail safe brake and I put the forty five ton steam crane in its place. Derby wanted the steam crane back so that they could swap it with the crane of another gang which was to have their crane dieselised. However, I wasn't going to let it go until I was fully satisfied with my big crane.

To test the fail safe brake, the crane was set up and I had a shunting loco hanging on the chains. It was only an inch off the rails and if the brake didn't work, the loco would only drop a small distance. To simulate the loss of hydraulic oil pressure one of the oil pipes was removed by the Derby fitters. The fail safe breaks were positioned on a shaft by the hydraulic motors either side of the crane and all they consisted of was a disk brake. The left hand side calliper worked but the right hand side one didn't. I had more problems now with the crane but I could pass them over to the Derby fitters and let them get on with them. They knew I wasn't happy.

Later that day we were called to Jones' Scrap sidings at Waltham Cross. A mineral wagon had derailed at trap points protecting the up main. It was a bit of a hurry up job as there was a danger that the scrap firm may cut up the wagon for extra scrap. It was often alleged that a string of ten mineral wagons loaded with scrap would be shunted into one of the larger scrap firms and only seven or eight shunted out. As it was adjacent to the main line we couldn't stand the train next to the job so, as soon as we were alongside, the lads scrambled into the tool van and threw out the hand jacks and packing that we would need and the train carried on to Broxbourne for the loco to run round and wait for us to call it back. We had probably re-railed the mineral wagon before the loco on the breakdown had finished running round at Broxbourne to haul the train back. I rang the signalman, and told him that we were ready to be picked up. The jacks and packing were positioned by the side of the up road and we waited a half hour. The train had barely stopped alongside us and all the equipment was stowed away. Then we were off back to the shed.

By the end of the month the Derby fitters had finished working on the diesel crane. They told me it was good, but I had my doubts.

I was invited to a site meeting at Ilford Station. There was to be a new foot bridge put up in place of the old cast iron one at the London end of the platforms. It was to take three weekends. At this time I was also told that the March gang would be getting a big diesel crane and I was to teach them on my crane and pass out the supervisor, Frank, and the crane driver, Reg. I said that I would and hoped my crane would be fit to use.

In September we were called to twenty three jobs. I had asked the Yard Manager in Temple Mills to save any trans-ship or reloading jobs until the end of the month if it was possible. It would be then that the March gang would be with us.

I had the big crane put in the train but held on to the forty five ton steam crane, just in case.

The March gang arrived and were to stay in a B.&.B. on the Romford Road. They had only used a forty five ton Cowans Sheldon built steam crane, so I had to start training them from the beginning. I explained how important it was to have the outriggers out and packed. As the weight of the jib slewed at ninety degrees, their new crane could be turned over if they were to lower the jib over the thirty feet radius. Another thing to remember was that there was an eighteen feet overhang at the back of the crane. I thought I had covered everything and we took the B.D.V. train down to Temple Mills Cattle Dock to continue 'on the job' training. With an array of wagons to be reloaded or trans-shipped, there was a week's work.

We also dealt with three derailments during daylight hours at the Mills. At 0300 hours on the 28th we were called to Stratford International Freight Terminal. Two loaded freight liner vehicles AGE601438 and AGE602594 were derailed and spread across the yard. We soon had the crane set up and the vehicles re-railed. As it was close to 0600 hours when we were ready to depart back to the shed, I had the guard take the train to the Cattle Dock and arranged for the March gang to come straight there. We had a full day trans-shipping and reloading.

That night, at 2030 hours, we were called to a couple of mineral wagons blocking F fan and then to the East Yard where an empty engineers' wagon had derailed. On our return to Stratford I decided not to go home as it was so late and I had a busy programme the next day.

I was hoping to pass out Reg, from the March gang and Ken from our gang. We started at 0800 hours and I had the March gang set up the crane by themselves. With just the one empty mineral wagon to play with, I had the two hopeful drivers, Reg and Ken, swinging the crane to left and right, lifting and lowering the jib and taking the mineral wagon up high above the New Shed. I had them drive in turns of thirty minutes each and I alternated the moves from slewing to the jib then the block quickly. Ken was working the crane well but when it was Reg's turn, I could hear Ken telling him what to do quietly through the tannoy. I had to take Ken out of the crane cab when Reg was driving. He was slower but did everything I asked of him. I gave them a hard time but they were both passed out at the end of the day. With the crane put away the two gangs were going to celebrate in the B.R.S.A. club. Then a call came for the Stratford gang to go to Marsh Lane to re-rail a mineral wagon similar to the one we had been playing with all day.

The following week I had Jim from March with us. He was the relief crane driver. He was a good old boy and talked very slowly. All the lads called him a real carrot cruncher. I had nothing prearranged for Jim but we attended seven derailments four of which were crane jobs. He was slow and steady and left Stratford with his certificate for driving the seventy five ton diesel crane.

In October we had twenty seven calls, most of which were at Temple Mills or Stratford but the first one was at Hartford East. A three car passenger unit had gone over the stops on number one platform. The cause was the slippery rails and the driver reported his wheels picking up on the unit. I had our loco 31103 tied on to the back of the unit and the air pipes connected, then pulled the unit off the top of the buffer stops and re-railed the leading bogie with hand jacks.

The reconstruction of foot bridge 78 at Ilford Station was getting closer. We would be needed on three weekends, starting on 7th October. The day before on 6th October we used the big crane on three derailments at Temple Mills without any bearings running hot or brakes failing. I hoped it would behave itself for the weekend.

We departed Stratford 2000 hours on the Saturday night and ran the short distance to Ilford. I had re-marshalled the breakdown train at the shed before we left and had the crane on the rear. On arrival at Ilford the breakdown train ran under the old bridge and stopped just passed it in the platform. We had to wait until the late trains had finished running, then the overhead line men could start slewing the wires. The reason it was going to take three weekends was because the bridge had three spans and the engineers only wanted to do one span each session. The old span was lifted down and loaded into a long engineers' wagon with low sides called a Tench. The cast iron pillars that held up the bridge were next to come down and they were loaded up along with the stair treads. We had a long wait whilst the train with the old bridge on it was shunted away and the new one brought alongside us.

By the time the engineers had prepared the footings for the new concrete pillars to be dropped in, it was 1500 hours. We started putting up the new concrete sections and had finished in two hours.

I was using the crane free on rail. That is without the outriggers being bedded down. There is always a risk that the foreman may forget the instability of the crane and lower the jib whilst the crane is slewed round. The engineers had asked me if I wanted the platform removing so I could set up the outriggers. As there was very little weight to be lifted and I had measured all the distances that the crane would have to jib out to, with nothing greater than thirty feet and most of the lifting over end, I told them not to bother. The first weekend was completed and the crane had performed well. The engineering staff told us how impressed they were with the diesel crane, never having to wait for the steam to be built up and a good bright light hanging from the jib, illuminating everything under the crane. I didn't tell them how worried I was about the crane failing. We arrived back at the shed at 2000 hours and I had the guard re-marshal the breakdown train before putting it in the New Shed.

We had six calls that next week and on the Friday night at 2350 we were called to Ripple Lane to assist them with two loaded oil tanks. The one hundred ton tanks were filled with a thick oil similar in consistency to bitumen and there was no chance of them catching fire, as it was such a cold night. With the job almost finished the last bogie was just above the rails and Ted started shouting over the tannoy that the jib was dropping. Everyone dived out of the way and the tank bogie slowly dropped on to the rails. It was 0700 hours Saturday morning and I had the centre span of the Ilford footbridge to put up that night. I still had the forty five ton steam crane, if I couldn't fix the big diesel. I had the crane put away and we went back to the shed. With John, Ted and Ken, I worked on the crane all morning checking the different brakes on it. One of the brackets that held the adjusting screw to the jib brake was loose and had some movement which caused the drum to slowly revolve whilst the brake was on. With that all tightened along with other bolts we found loose, I thought it would be fit to work on the foot bridge. I wasn't happy with the work that had been done at Derby on the crane, and concocted a letter to that effect.

We departed at 2000 hours that night to Ilford and the foot bridge job was uneventful, and we completed what we were asked to do. The lads as well as myself were very wary of the crane.

On the Monday our second call to Temple Mills was at 1930 hours. A string of loaded hoppers had come over the retarder and hadn't been slowed down. They ran the full length of the yard and came to grief when they collided with a string of tanks that was being pulled out of the yard on converging roads. Hoppers, tanks and a "van fit" were on their sides just by Ruckholt Road Bridge. It took us over three hours with the crane to clear the mess.

On Friday 20th October, Frank, the supervisor from March, came down to be passed out on the seventy five ton diesel crane. He had two drivers certificated and as soon as he was, too, his new crane would be delivered.

We had a couple of mineral wagons to trans-ship at the Cattle Dock and I let Frank get on with the job. I could see what was going on through the back windows in my office in the riding van and, as he was working with the best breakdown gang in the country, I knew that he would be fine. At 1300 hours the job was finished and we all departed to The Thatched House for lunch.

I discussed with Frank some of the finer points of the new diesel crane he would be getting.

One of the things we always had to do after a move was, whether slewing, roping or derricking, take the gear out and run everything in reverse. This had to be done to ensure that the gear that had been used was out before the next gear was chosen. By doing this it made sure that two gears were not in mesh at the same time. Another thing to point out was that the crane was perfectly balanced when the jib was at thirty feet radius. Without anything on the hook the crane could be safely slewed round 360 degrees and it was not necessary to set up the outriggers.

Frank returned to March with his certificate and was a happy man, looking forward to getting his big crane.

On 21st October we finished renewing the foot bridge at Ilford and the crane had performed as it should. We returned to Stratford New Shed at 2100 Sunday night.

On the Tuesday of the next week at 0127 hours, three empty gas oil tanks, 45027, 45097 and 51830 were derailed and over on their sides on the main line between Temple Mills and High Meads. The fire brigade were called but just stood by watching. The job was completed in two and a half hours with the big crane.

On the following weekend I took a couple of the lads who weren't booked on in the shed to Broxbourne. We had to spray paint the asbestos in the lift shafts on the station. So as not to frighten any of the public, as we wore our blue asbestos overalls and masks, we took all the equipment onto the roof and changed into our asbestos gear out of sight. We then entered the lift winding room and worked our way down the lift shaft spraying from the top of the lift. All the walls would be painted and we would drop the lift five or six feet and start again. We had a good system working and on the Sunday afternoon when none of the public were about we would finish the bottom of the shaft with the lift above us. We did many lift shafts in the next twelve months at Ilford, Romford and Chelmsford on the Colchester line and, on the Cambridge line, we worked at Harlow and Bishops Stortford, as well as Broxbourne.

In November we covered thirty jobs. On 2nd November we had three and the last one was at Harlow Mill in the Key Glass Works sidings. A hopper B886846 had run away and derailed all wheels at catch points protecting a road. The rail track went across a road and had hand operated crossing gates. When a train was being pushed in or pulled out of the glass works sidings, the guard had to shut the gates to road traffic and take the train over the crossing then open the gates for the road vehicles to cross. It was quite a busy road and the catch points, by derailing the hopper, had stopped what could have been a nasty accident. All the equipment had to be carried across the road to the derailed hopper which was loaded with soda ash used in the making of glass.

I remember the ground being very boggy and all the hand jacks and packing were covered in mud. The hopper was back on the track and manually pushed back into the glass works and secured. The dirty equipment was loaded on to a P Way trolley and taken back to the breakdown train. As we were loading the train we found a broken spring on the crane and had to change that before our return to Stratford.

On 5th November at 2045 hours we were called to the country end of Hockley Station on the Southend line. An engineers' train had propelled back through catch points derailing a guards brake 954053, a Catfish DB983632, a Mackerel DB992266 and a

Sturgeon DB994100. Two hours after arriving all the offending wagons were re-railed using hand jacks and the B.D.V. ran through to Southend to run the loco round to the back of the train and make our way back to Stratford.

On 7th November we had three calls. The first was at Temple Mills. A loco 31019 was derailed number two bogie. That was put on and we went to Broxbourne. Two hoppers B417255 and E303682 were derailed in the up sidings behind the signal box. We had lunch in the Kingfisher and returned to the Mills to re-rail a pair of mineral wagons.

On our return to the shed the Chief Clerk met us and informed us that Derby Works wanted the seventy five ton diesel crane back to do more work on it. Before the lads went home we changed over the outrigger packing and chains from ADB966111 to the steam crane 330133 again.

The following day we started at 0525 hours. Ted had been warming up the steam crane during the night and it was back in the train in place of the diesel crane. The call was to the Stratford Freight Liner Terminus. Shunting loco 08407 was pulling a string of freight liner wagons and ran through catch points protecting the main line, derailing itself and the first vehicle 601062. I had our train stand on the main line with the crane next to the job. The lads were setting up the crane and Ted was getting up steam. The job started well and the freight liner wagon was re-railed in minutes. We started to work on the shunting loco and had the chains positioned to lift the rear. I was going to do it with two lifts as the shunting loco weighs fifty tons, first the rear and then the front.

When I shouted to Ted to take the weight, nothing happened. He was having trouble with the gears. John climbed up onto the foot plate to help but between them they were unable to get the rope drum to work. We could slew and take the jib up and down but were unable to get any movement on the rope. The curse of the crane had struck again. I decided to continue the job with the M.F.D. We would work on the crane when we had finished the re-railing. The train had to be moved so that the M.F.D. van was opposite the job. Using the 120/60 ton jacks we soon had the front end on and we were setting up at the rear of the loco to finish the job.

A load of men in suits and very clean high visibility vests came on to site. It seems they were travelling with the new Chairman on the railway, Sir Peter Parker. They told me that my breakdown train was blocking the path of the rail car that all the dignitaries were travelling in and asked me if Sir Peter could come and see the job we were doing. I thought it a silly request as he was after all the chairman. He came down to site and we shook hands. He was interested in the job, why it had happened, and how we were dealing with it.

I soon had the shunting loco re-railed and then had our breakdown train shunted into the Freight Liner Terminus to clear the main line.

Sir Peter Parker was doing a tour of the sheds in the London area and went passed us towards Stratford.

We still had the jib up on the crane and with big hammers and long bars we managed to get the gear to the rope drum engaged and drop the block to get the chains off and then put the block to the top of the jib. The jib was lowered on to the jib carrier and the crane was put away. We then made our way back to the shed.

As we were running down six road towards the New Shed, the crane struck a diamond crossing and became derailed one pair of wheels. The lads started to get the hand jacks out and I went to the office to let the signalman know not to put anything down that part of the shed.

As I entered the office there was Sir Peter talking to the other foremen. I was very embarrassed as I made my call to the Bobby and quickly made my way back to the crane. The gang had put it back on the track and the guard was preparing to knock it out of the train. We worked all afternoon on the gears and found grease nipples that had never seen grease since they had been fitted. Ted was getting the gears in and out freely, so I thought the crane could be put back into the train.

The crane was picked up the next day at 0700 hours when we went to Bishops Stortford. A loco 31005 was derailed all wheels at points to the coal road on the Down Sidings. We completed the job and, as we were returning to Stratford, I was looking through the back windows of my office and I saw smoke coming from the left hand side of the crane. I had a hot box on the crane. We were just outside Stratford so I had the train run gently into the shed and had the driver and guard knock out the crane and put it to one side to be worked on.

I checked all the axle boxes and it was the right hand rear box that was hot. The bearing must have moved when the wheels struck the diamond. I told the O.D.M. and asked the C&W if they had any new bearings and pads for our crane and that I would be working on it the next day. But on the next day the 10th, we were called at 0120 to go to Harlow Mill. A loco 37075 had derailed all wheels at buffer stops in the yard.

The loco had pushed the stops back over thirty feet and was buried in muck up to its axles. It was a cold wet miserable morning and, as there was no urgency, we took our time with the M.F.D. With the loco back on the good bit of track we made our way back to Stratford. We were without a crane. The big diesel was going to Derby and the little steamer was no good because of the hot box. The breakdown train was berthed in the New Shed in the early afternoon.

A carriage and wagon fitter had been removing all the bearings and oil pads from the axle boxes. I checked them with him. The bearings were twelve by seven inches in size and a new one would be required for the right hand rear axle box. All the oil pads could do with renewing. The fitter promised me he would find a new bearing and bring it and new pads first thing the next day.

If he had no luck with the bearing, the old one would have to go away to be re-metalled, and that would take time.

The next day was Armistice Day and the C&W fitter had turned up trumps. He had found a new bearing that was the right size and brought eight new pads with him. Just to explain, the bearing fits inside the top of the axle box and rests on the top of the axle sticking out from the wheel. A carriage spring sits on the top of the box and takes the weight of the vehicle. On the steam crane there are eight in all on the carriage. The bearings are made of brass and have a white metal covering inside the curve that comes into contact with the axle.

In the bottom of the box sits the sprung pad in a well of oil. The oil is soaked into the pad which is pressed up against the bottom of the axle and, as the axle turns, it rotates across the oily pad and is constantly lubricated.

When fitting a new pad it is wise to make sure that the pad is well pregnated with oil and the best way to do this is to boil up a bucket of oil with the pad in it. As we had eight pads they were put in a half barrel of oil and heated up.

I had O.D.M. fitters working with some of the breakdown lads on the gears and the rest of my gang were helping the C&W fitters. To remove a bearing the axle box has to be jacked up and the weight taken off the axle. As we were doing this I noticed that some of the springs had more weight on them than others.

By 1400 hours all the work on the crane was completed and I had it shunted back into the train.

I knew that Derby had a mobile wheel weight comparator, for checking the weight of an individual wheel whilst it was in the vehicle. I rang them and asked if I could borrow it to weigh each axle on the steam crane. I also wanted to know how my seventy five ton crane was coming on. I was told that the wheel comparator would be dispatched to me as soon as possible and the big crane would soon be on its way back to me.

The wheel weight comparator arrived. It was in a wooden box, and had an oily paper with instructions on it stapled to the lid. The comparator was about eighteen inches long, four inches wide and two inches deep. At each end, sticking out at right angles, was a four inch square block that held a small jack. In the middle of the comparator was a hand pump, with a short handle and a clock gauge. The whole assembly would be placed on the rail with the blocks on either side of the wheel that was to be checked. The two small jacks worked off the one pump. I would pump the two jacks up until they were touching the wheel. A long feeler gauge was slid along the rail until it was resting against the wheel. After each stroke with the pump handle, I would try to pass the feeler gauge under the wheel and, as soon as that happened, I would take the reading on the clock gauge and note it down. The gauge wasn't in tons but in pounds per square inch. When all the wheels had been checked, I had eight readings. All the readings were totally different but should have been similar. The system written on the lid of the wooden box told the operator how many flats to turn on the nuts on the hanger bolts to increase or decrease the weight. I tried this method and the springs were worse than when I started. It took me two days before I had the springs pulled down as they should be.

On 16th November we received a call to Ilford New Dock. The New Dock was on the opposite side to the Carriage Sidings. It was on the up side of the main line. Three milk tanks B3176, W1976 and W1955 had been shunted heavily onto the stops and all three had derailed. We couldn't stand the train next to the job as it would mean blocking the main line. The breakdown train had to stop inside the Carriage Sidings and the hand jacks and packing were carried across the tracks to the job. All the tanks were soon re-railed and we returned to Stratford.

The big crane had been brought back to Stratford and, as I still had the wheel comparator, I checked all the wheels and found many discrepancies. No wonder the springs were breaking.

I reset all the weights on the springs and had our crane put back into the breakdown train. I had been even busier working on the two cranes and attending to the minor derailments in Temple Mills.

On 24th November we started at 0440 hours in the Mills at the Manor End. Two loaded tanks, ALG 49097 and ALG 49120 had run away and met a string of six empty wagons, hitting them on converging roads. The tanks stayed upright but the empty wagons fared much worse and most were turned over. We used the big diesel crane and within two hours all the vehicles were back on the tracks. We departed to the East Yard, leaving the C&W working on the wagons to get them runnable.

We had a guards brake over the buffer stops in the East Yard. After that was dealt with, we returned to the hump end of H fan where a mineral wagon and a "high fit" had derailed. We were just arriving back at Stratford outlet when we were called back to C fan in the Mills. Two loaded mineral wagons B580409 and B562265 had become lock buffered in the middle of a train. All the work was finished and we were back in the New Shed by 1600 hours.

We used the big crane twice more before the end of November and it seemed to be working well.

In December we only had nineteen calls up to Christmas and every one was in Temple Mills. Three were shunting locos and the rest were mineral wagons, tanks or hoppers. On 16th we had three jobs starting at 0700 hours in H fan number two road. Staying in H fan, three loaded mineral wagons had derailed on number six road. We were just putting them back on when we saw a string of tanks hurtle down the hump, over the retarder and collide with a string of wagons, derailing two of them. We were back in the shed by midday.

With four derailments between Christmas Day and New Years Eve, the weather was very cold with an occasional blizzard. The last two derailments of the year were caused by snow in the points and it looked as if it was going to be a bad start to 1979.